To SHEL —

MY FRIEND, THE FAMILY MAN.
NOT THE SHELDON I KNEW
BUT ONE I STILL LOVE.

sleeping with your
gynecologist

sleeping with your gynecologist

Tales from my marriage to an OB/GYN

Marc Jaffe

WEST ST JAMES PRESS

Published by
West St. James Press
13938A Cedar Rd., #292
University Hts., OH 44118-3204
877-386-6936

Printed in the United States

Distributed by Seven Hills Book Distributors

ISBN 0-9672818-0-6

Library of Congress Catalog Card Number 99-96607

Book Design by Anne Fahey
Cover Design by Michael Anthony Lynch

for my girls,
Alena, Jana, and Sarah
AND THEIR FRIEND SAM

Contents

Playing Doctor ▪ The Doctor's Wife ▪ Self-Helpless ▪ My Daughter-in-law the Doctor ▪ Call Me Anytime ▪ It's 4 a.m., Do You Know What Time It Is? ▪ Don't I Know You? ▪ Office Hours ▪ Handywoman ▪ Perks

They Only Serve Those Who Wait ▪ Making Babies ▪ Diploma . . . tic ▪ Could You Please Pass the . . . Eww ▪ Doctor Approved ▪ Nervous Wreck ▪ Crime and Punishment ▪ Bad . . . umm . . . Timing ▪ Tattoos and Body Piercing ▪ Lunchtime is Drugtime ▪ Condomania ▪ You Put What? Where? ▪ Return To Sender ▪ The Password Is . . . ▪ Movies of the Week ▪ Table for Two ▪ Miss-Conception ▪ Last Patient of the Day

Introduction

The first thing I want to make clear is that I am not a doctor. I wanted to be one. I lacked only two of the requisites for becoming a physician: talent and effort. Four years of med school and another four in residency seemed like too much to invest. For what? A career? Besides, that application looked a little complicated.

I doubt I would have gotten into med school had I applied. Med schools take the best and the brightest. I was average and flickering. And the fact that seeing sick people makes me uneasy and my legs quiver would not bode well for a future in medicine.

Yet here I am holding myself out as a medical expert. How can I do this? I married into it. Granted, that doesn't quite give me the expertise to impart advice that an education and experience would provide, but then doctors usually write such dry, boring books that no one can get through to take advantage of the worthwhile advice. I thought I'd write an honest, funny book that doesn't give advice. I won't cure any of your ailments, but I hope you will forget about them for a while.

So if this book has no advice, what does it offer? It gives you a chance to see into the day-to-day life of a typical OB/GYN. If you got as far as I did on your way to becoming a doctor, this will serve as an insight into what your life might have been like. If you are simply a woman who wants to know what it's like on the other side of the speculum, then this book will give you that view. If you are just looking for reassurance that other patients are as clueless and as embarrassed as you are about everything from having a baby to having a Pap smear—that is provided. If you think an experience of yours might be in here . . . hey . . . remember, it's all in good fun.

Let me repeat that last part—it's all in good fun. Sure, some patients will appear idiotic in these stories. That doesn't mean they aren't otherwise bright, wonderful people. But who is going to laugh at a book of stories about a trip to the gynecologist where the patients are all smart and everything goes according to plan? Only publishers, when you present them with the idea.

Similarly, while I tried to include as many stories of doctor's errors as I could, their mistakes often led to less than humorous conclusions. A doctor who doesn't know about electricity is pretty funny to an electrician. We all play someone's fool. It's acceptable as long as it's not in your own profession. A doctor who doesn't know about medicine is plain scary.

So please accept any perceived ridicule of patients as coming from an equally befuddled peer. I too am less than fully informed about my own body. I make diagnoses of personal ailments based on magazine articles. *People Magazine*. Remedies come from the checkout woman at the drugstore who tells me what worked for her. And when I do manage to visit the doctor, I accept only his wisdom that is convenient. Just because he went to med school doesn't mean I have to believe him when he gives that mumbo jumbo about my weight gain being a result of my diet. Preposterous!

While I may be able to relate to my readers as health-seeking compatriots, I cannot share the experience of having gone to an OB/GYN. Had I been married to a urologist, this wouldn't have been an issue. As a man, I can make fun of other men and, by inference, all maledom, as long as I remind you how lovable we really are. Will women give me the same leeway? I hope so. These stories are told about women only because it is women who have babies and visit the gynecologist. I respect women. I admire women. I can't say I fully understand them, but that shouldn't prevent me from listening and observing and writing about what I see and hear. And let me add—women are lovable.

In addition to giving the general public a view from the white coats, there is another reason I wrote this book. That is, to give my wife a break from telling about her life and all the funny stories that happen to her. Every get-together we are in, be it a class or social gathering, eventually breaks down into Karen entertaining the group with chronicles of her daily existence. She is in a monthly book club and returns home each time to tell me how they discussed the selected book for a while until, before she knew it, she was holding court on reproductive matters. Karen is a well-rounded, interesting person. She would like to talk about something else for a change. Instead of Karen's life being a chapter at the end of every book club, I figured I'd make it a whole book, and then the club can move on to something else.

As many good yarns as Karen has, however, it wasn't quite enough to fill a book. So I interviewed dozens of doctors, midwives and nurses to get all these stories, and I want to thank them all for their time and contributions. All the stories in this book are true, to the best of my knowledge. Unless some of those doctors are making things up. Some stories—like the one about the 60-something woman who unknowingly used her granddaughter's "Barbie sparkle hairspray" to freshen up with before her annual exam—couldn't be corroborated. In that story, the doctor went to examine her and saw the sparkles and commented, "My, aren't we special today!" I heard that story from a couple of doctors who all said it happened to a friend of a friend, leading to my suspicion that it may have happened once, but is now an urban gynecological legend.

Let me assure you that in all my research, privacy was maintained. No doctor ever told me a patient's name, so if you recognize your circumstances in one of the narratives, trust that neither I nor any readers know who you are.

That such a high percentage of doctors whom I asked to contribute were willing to do so was encouraging. Some members of the medical profession can be a bit averse to humor. I understand that health care is a very serious matter. That doesn't mean funny things don't happen. We don't need lots of OBs secretly placing their foot on the scale as pregnant women are getting weighed. We can let my wife be the only mischievous doctor to do that. (Don't worry, she eventually tells them.) But my personal choice would be to be cared for by a doctor with a sense of humor. I was glad to have met so many.

Surely I'm prejudiced when I say that no doctor I met had such a finely tuned sense of humor as my wife, Karen. I am blessed to have her as my partner. I use the term partner in many ways. As husband and wife we are joined in love and fortune. As parents of three amazing daughters, we are a team. A team that on occasion even wins. And now, by virtue of this book, we are professional partners as well. In writing this book, I have come to better appreciate Karen's gifts as a doctor. She is almost universally admired by her patients and peers, and I share in the admiration of the good works she does. Patients are comforted by Karen's confidence and compassion. What few patients see, however, is Karen's humility and, tipping of the scales aside, her wonderful sense of humor about herself. If she is your doctor, you should feel lucky. I know I feel lucky to be sleeping with your gynecologist.

— *Marc Jaffe*

THE DOCTOR DISROBES

An OB's Home Life Revealed

Playing Doctor

My wife just delivered a baby.

Usually that statement brings on a flurry of congratulations and cheap cigars, but in this case it's no big deal. She delivers a baby, on average, a couple of times a week.

My wife is an obstetrician/gynecologist.

That fact was omitted in a recent issue of her college alumni magazine. Karen had written in to tell about her life, which included a husband, three kids and a fulfilling career in the baby business. Through poor editing, the entry read, "Karen Jaffe writes that she is married and has three kids and loves delivering babies." They neglected to mention that she was an obstetrician. It sounded like she was some kind of well-oiled birthing machine. She just loooves pushing out those babies. As if hardly a day goes by when she doesn't tell someone "Gosh, I can't think of anything more fun than a few hours of contractions and then ripping myself open to deliver a little one. Damn that nine-month gestation period, otherwise I could have a kid every day."

That's not to say that she wasn't grateful to have delivered her own children. Again, the English language forces me to clarify. She didn't professionally deliver her own children. There was another doctor there handling the delivery.

That she may have performed physician duties during her own deliveries is a surprisingly common assumption people make when they find out she's an OB. If people would consider the possible complications, they wouldn't make that assumption. It's not like my wife would be able to perform her own C-section. She didn't have a scalpel nearby, ready to cut herself open and yank out the baby just before collapsing like Rambo in the wilderness carving a bullet out of his leg so he can jump back into the fray. No. She had another doctor there.

Admittedly her relationship with her doctor was a bit different than most women have with their doctors. Most women in labor ask questions, try to verbalize their feelings and wishes, look to their doctors for guidance. Karen gave orders.

"Cut the f—ing episiotomy!" was, I believe the most decisive order she gave her doctor.

Most of the time leading up to that point they talked shop. In some sense it was a relief that my wife had a handle on the situation. Kind of like taking your car to get the clutch fixed, knowing your spouse is a certified auto mechanic. Only, of course, having a baby is cheaper.

The comfort that Karen's professional knowledge afforded me was offset by my exclusion due to my inability to understand the lingo. I had no idea what was going on during any of the delivery. She's yakking away with the doctor in medicalese that might as well have been Spanish for all I knew. I felt like I was watching a Spanish news broadcast where every now and then an English word would come up and capture my attention.

This is what a typical exchange between my wife, her doctor and me sounded like to a non-medical/non-Spanish speaking layman:

DOCTOR: Karen, *nos fuentes primas de todo los cochitores mucho fastidore para viejas con* SAMMY DAVIS *no mas.*

KAREN: *Despues lampilona en su bajadores de* PLACENTA. (They laugh)

ME: What? What's happening? All I understood was "Sammy Davis" and "placenta." Does the placenta show the child needs a glass eye? Does the candy man make placenta candies? Someone please explain how you got placenta and Sammy Davis in the same conversation.

KAREN (calming voice): Don't worry. We were just talking about this anesthesiology resident whose name is Sam Davis, but he looks nothing like the singer. He's a slimy guy, so we gave him the nickname "Placenta" which (turning to doctor), *Como se dice en ingles* "placenta"? Oh yeah, big, slimy thing. That's all. Nothing to worry about, dear.

Granted, most professions have their own lingo that excludes outsiders, but none is more intimidating than the medical profession. That's because of the enormity of the consequences when health is the issue. Using the lingo allows doctors to take even more control of the situation. My wife uses this to her full advantage. Early in her first pregnancy she complained of some pain. I asked her what she thought it was. She said she was sure it was "round ligament pain." "Round ligament pain" sounds a lot more serious than "a pain in my side." I was concerned. I asked her, what we should do? She became very clinical and said, "Well, I need to rest, and you need to clean the house."

My lack of medical knowledge is only a part of the parcel of inadequacy I feel relative to our professions. On any given day, I can ask my wife what she did, and she might go into a five-minute story of how there was some mother with ". . . pre-eclampsia/bradicardia, blah blah blah . . . yada yada . . . and WE SAVED THE WOMAN'S LIFE!"

When your spouse saves someone's life, how do you, with any sense of self-worth, respond to the inevitable, "And how was your day?"

"Umm, well, I wrote a joke . . . and I went to the cleaners. So I did two things there. That cleaners, boy, that's a trip . . . ."

I get great satisfaction out of knowing that my wife does on occasion save a life. I've never actually seen her do it, but I trust that she has. I've never even seen her do a delivery or perform a surgery. I'd like to. She won't let me. Partially out of respect for the patients. I think most women are resigned to the fact that a group of people is going to be looking at their genitals during the birth, but when non-medical people start coming in "just to see," that would be especially unnerving.

I don't really want to see a regular birth anyway. I want to see a C-section. It's not the operation itself that interests me. For that I can turn on the Surgery Channel. (Thursday nights—Must see vasectomy.) What I want to see is Karen wielding a knife, slicing into someone, calling for surgical instruments. I want to see the woman I love, the woman who is grossed out by a pus blister, calmly deal with blood and innards as she rattles off one-liners and pithy remarks to the amusement of her fellow doctors. I'm just assuming she operates like a female Hawkeye Pierce.

Be aware that she doesn't usually rattle off one-liners and pithy remarks in day-to-day life, but I assume she would do it in the operating room because that is my only experience seeing doctors operate. If that's not the way it is, then let me see the truth. I CAN HANDLE THE TRUTH! (I was doing my best Jack Nicholson impression there.) The only truth I see is that my wife is too nervous to perform in front of an audience.

She used to get nervous when I performed standup comedy. Just the thought that I might not be funny kept her away from the clubs. I tried to explain that I do it every week with great success, I was good at it, and if by some chance I failed on that night, then the worst that could happen would be that I'd die on stage and walk away with a slightly bruised ego, ready to go back at it again the next day. She would take a deep breath and consent to accompany me.

I used the same argument in trying to get to see her perform.

"Karen, you do this every week with great success, you're good at it, and if by some chance you fail, then the worst that could happen would be that someone would die on the table and you'd walk away with a slightly bruised ego and a large malpractice suit, ready to go back at it again the next day."

Like I said, I have yet to see her operate.

What I have seen is the preparation before the operation—the hard work that goes on the night before she has a scheduled procedure. That's when Karen brings her manuals and textbooks to bed. Keeping romance in a marriage is difficult, and bringing work to bed doesn't lend to an amorous atmosphere. That's true even when the work is pictures of women's genitalia.

As any eighth-grade teacher who has shown the state-produced sex films will attest, seeing the reproductive system up close will quell any interest in sex pretty quickly. Seeing diseased or deformed reproductive parts can make you swear off sex for days at a time. Most of the pictures that I glimpse are of inflamed uteruses or bloody fibroids the size of bocci balls. Why spend money on birth control when you can just open up to page 576 of *Gynecologic and Obstetric Surgery.*

Some of you are probably thinking, "Wait a minute, she still references her textbooks? Aren't doctors supposed to know this stuff by the time they start practicing?"

No.

Doctors know the common things they see day to day, but give them some slightly off-kilter disease and it has them scrambling for the textbooks. I should think you would be thankful if your doctor boned up on a procedure before performing it. Obviously the best thing is to get a doctor who has performed your particular surgery hundreds of times before doing it on you. If they haven't, don't fret. A little brushing up and they should do a great job. Now, what you don't want to see is your doctor consulting her textbook at the side of the table during surgery, mumbling about a part that didn't seem to be included in the kit.

That's why they have anesthesia—so you don't see that. They have malpractice insurance in case you do see it. Not that *you* would sue over something so benign, but there are plenty of people who would.

The whole idea of being sued is very scary to doctors. Imagine that in your job, you did something every day that had the potential for a lawsuit that could wipe out your entire net worth. It would make you a little more cautious. Might change the way you work. Might leave you cowering in a corner unable to function. Yet your OB is out there everyday, delivering babies, while those scum-sucking lawyers hover, lurking, circling like vultures waiting for one little slip-up to claim millions for bogus pain and suffering . . . I may not be completely objective on this.

The Doctor's Wife

In the early days of Karen's practice, we considered what would happen if she got sued. So now, to avoid losing all our accumulated savings and wealth in the event of some bad delivery—I own everything. I own the house. I own the cars. I own the stocks and bonds. I am all for this.

Just because I own everything, don't think that being a kept man is all beer and pretzels. I have gone through much soul-searching to deal with the fact that most years, Karen makes more money than me. O.K., every year. See, I've come to grips with it. I don't have to make all the money to be the provider. I contribute in other ways. I take the kids to school, to swimming lessons, skating lessons and birthday parties. I do the grocery shopping and cooking. I do laundry . . . cleaning . . . volunteer . . . at . . . school. My God, I'm the wife!

I can accept that. Wifedom is a noble profession. It's not like I've lost my identity. I kept my own name when we got married. How's that for independence? And I convinced Karen to take my name despite the fact that she was already established professionally. This way, if she ever invents something or discovers a disease, the Jaffe name could be immortalized. I envision patients being brought in for a Jaffeoscopy.

To be honest, Karen was thrilled to take my name. It took no persuasion on my part. She was not very fond of her maiden name—Regan. In addition, she is a very practical and far-seeing individual. She realized the future ramifications that many of today's identity-preserving couples haven't thought about—tombstones. Had she not changed her name, we would have had to have an addendum put on our tombstones explaining our being laid to rest side by side. I picture arrows carved into the rocks pointing in each other's direction with the inscriptions: "Marc Jaffe—Karen Regan: They were married."

As happy as she is to have my name, she will in no way accept my use of her title. I never claim to be a doctor, but sometimes we get mail addressed to "Dr. and Mrs. Jaffe." That sets her off into a tirade about having spent four years at med school plus another four in residency just so she could be called doctor, and some clerk goes and makes a common assumption that just goes to show how society is prejudiced . . . and on and on until I finally interrupt her and say, "Fine, we won't enter the Publishers' Clearinghouse Sweepstakes if you feel that strongly about it."

It's not just faceless mega-mailers that think I'm the doctor of the house. The local institutions—the museums or nature center where we have a membership—are often confused by our prefixes. I will sign up for a "Mommy and me" class—known in our family as a "Mommy can't make it and me" class—and I won't think to clarify things when signing up. Either the class list is then printed wrong, or the teacher won't pay close enough attention. I am made conscious of the misunderstanding when invariably some medical issue comes up and the instructor turns to me for enlightenment. For example, the naturalist will be talking about mosquitoes and mention that she thinks that when they bite they inject some heparin into us to clot the blood. Then she will look to me for confirmation. Instead of just agreeing , I admit that I don't know what heparin is, and instantly a dozen mommies whisper to their kids, "That's why we go to a different doctor."

Thankfully, I have yet to be in a situation where I am expected to perform some medical heroism just because my title has been written incorrectly. I'm waiting for the clichéd experience of being in a theater when an emergency arises and a man steps to the microphone and asks if there is a doctor in the house. Everyone will look at me, and I'll have to correct them. "I am not a doctor!" Then, desperate for help they'll cry, "Is there anyone married to a doctor in the house?" In which case I'll have no excuse not to perform surgery.

Now that we've established that I'm not a doctor, what is my title? I do have a degree. Got my MBA. Got it in a drawer somewhere at my parents' house. It says I'm a "Master of Business Administration." Well, the only business I'm administrating is the Jaffe family, and trust me, I am not its master. I think the common term for what I do is "house-husband." Personally, I don't mind being called that, it's just that many still see it as a suspect lifestyle. See, even in this age when over 99% of women work outside the home,* I usually find myself as the lone male as I go about my shopping, skating lessons etc. And being the lone male is not an enviable position. I am questioned. I am looked at askew. I am talked about. I am paranoid, I'll grant you that, but even if they aren't talking about me, they definitely aren't talking *to* me. Oh sure, there are the friendly hellos and small talk about the weather and the kids, but the second another mom comes over, I'm tossed aside like egg whites in a mayonnaise. (I told you I do the cooking.)

I guess they feel they understand each other in ways that I never could. After all, I am a man. And, to be honest, I don't really want to be in their conversation. I don't like to converse. After all, I am a man. My patrilineage is a series of strong silent types. The men in my family can trace the family tree back over 30 generations to a gang of mute weightlifters in Lithuania. That's how strong and silent we are. So, let them exclude me. Chances are they are talking about their gynecologist.

I am not emasculated by my predicament. Rather, my man-

*Based on a survey of women working in Karen's office

liness is reinforced. By my own proclamation I have become male guardian of the neighborhood. During the day, when all the other men are at work, I am the male presence. All the wives on the street come to me when their plumbing fails or a heavy box needs to be moved or a rodent is found in the basement. I'm a chore gigolo, and the women I serve are satisfied.

One week, another husband took off from work and spent time around the house. I felt my job as defender of the neighborhood maidens had been usurped. I had to protect my turf. I challenged him to a duel. He accepted my challenge. We drank beers and had a belching contest. I don't remember who won, it was just good to communicate with a man again.

Self-Helpless

If current trends continue, I will be seeing more men out and about during my daytime excursions. These men will be former OB/GYNs who have lost their patient base to the recent abundance of female physicians. Karen finds this sad, as some excellent doctors are struggling from what amounts to sex discrimination. In her view, the societal change doesn't have to right the wrongs of past generations, when women doctors were almost unheard of. She doesn't want a backlash against men, but she is glad people don't call her "nurse." That was still a problem during her residency, when she would go into a room and the patient would ask her for the bedpan. Karen would say, "I'm DOCTOR Jaffe." A not-so-subtle way of saying, "It's not my job." The patient would apologize and ask again, like the hospital had some sort of Simon Sez policy, "O.K., DOCTOR Jaffe, can I have the bedpan?" Karen would pocket her degree and hand them the bedpan because, hey, when you gotta go . . . .

The prevailing attitude is that a woman doctor will be able to relate better to a woman's needs and problems. Even when choosing among female doctors, many women will say that one of the deciding factors in choosing my wife was the fact that she had children. They think that this will help her be a better doctor when it comes to their pregnancy.

Karen accepts them as patients but finds it a strange criterion for choosing a doctor. After all, you don't choose a dermatologist because he gets a lot of warts. Should you, God forbid, need your arm amputated, you wouldn't look for a doctor with no arms.

Whatever it is that patients seek in an OB/GYN, they seem to find it with Karen. She has a very busy practice. In fact it's full. She has the luxury of refusing patients. Any rejections are based purely on the numbers. There is no discrimination based on race, creed, color or sex. Strike that, she does discriminate by sex. If she had her choice, she would also discriminate by having only calm, healthy patients who don't know too much. Education is a fine thing as long as it doesn't come from self-help books and Lamaze classes.

Lamaze must provide some benefit. I'm not sure what it is, because I never went. It's a couples' thing, and my wife figured there was no point in her going and disrupting the class with her hysterical laughter every time the instructor tried to convince the class that proper BREATHING would get you through the pain. I find it somewhat dubious, considering that everyone is at Lamaze for their first baby. No one goes for subsequent deliveries. If it was so helpful, wouldn't people want to brush up?

The self-help books are only marginally better. They give a sensible foundation but tend to sugarcoat things. I have yet to find a book entitled *Childbirth: This is Really Going to Hurt*. Worse, they give a false sense that things are orderly, and that a mother should be following a norm. If everything doesn't go according to the book, patients get all panicky. "I'm in week 34 and I'm not making excessive trips to the bathroom. Something must be terribly wrong!"

Relax. It's not gospel. Just the other day I was reading *What to Expect in the 40th Year* and it says that this month I will pull a hamstring and finally pay off those college loans. Well, I know that it I've got at least another six months before those loans get paid off, but do you see me running to my internist? No. Not with my bad hamstring. I may sue the publisher, but I'm not bothering my doctor.

My Daughter-in-law, the Doctor

There is a percentage of patients who seem to have garnered a degree in pharmacology without actually attending any formal school. They walk in and simply tell the doctor that they need this drug or that drug. These patients are known as relatives. My parents, her sisters, everyone thinks it's great that they have a doctor for a relative. Get sick, call Karen for antibiotics. She will protest that what they have will not be cured by antibiotics, that it's viral and by taking antibiotics they are helping to promote drug-resistant bacteria. Her protests have little effect, and when it comes to choosing between a pissed-off father-in-law and the eventual fate of mankind . . . well, let's just say the world is a little less safe because of it.

It's not just drugs that are sought by her friends and relatives. It's doctor's notes too. Excuses for missing school, work or, most importantly, airplane flights when there is a non-refundable ticket involved. Karen tries to avoid doing that for my father by mumbling something about mandatory jail terms for those caught and suggesting that a sharp airline employee might just question why a man needed emergency fibroid surgery.

I am guilty of abusing her professional standing as well. I don't ask for things. I simply offer her services. Whenever friends from out of town call to let me know that they are pregnant, I tell them that they are welcome to call Karen anytime with questions. She cringes when she hears this. For some ethical reason she doesn't like giving advice to patients she's never met. I figure I'm just being neighborly. It's the medical equivalent of "Let's do lunch." I never really expect anyone to actually call and have lunch.

Well, some people do call. They never want to bother Karen, but their doctor is "unavailable" for a couple of days. What doctor is unavailable? There are pagers and cell phones and backups when the doctor is on vacation. I've never known a practice not to have some contact person every minute of the year, but apparently those practices exist. A patient calls and gets a recording saying, "The doctor isn't here, I hope you have a friend who's a gynecologist."

I suspect that what they are really calling for is a second opinion. Trust me on this: Nothing good can come from a second opinion. If Karen agrees with her doctor, then everything is hunky dory—except that our friend is stuck with the original bad news. On the other hand, if she gives a different diagnosis, what does our friend do? See which doctor went to the more prestigious med school? Get a third bid and take the middle one? Have Karen and her regular doctor duke it out? Somehow my "let's do lunch" leads to opening a can of worms, and that's not a culinary experience I enjoy. From now on I'll try to keep my mouth shut.

I'm not the only one guilty of volunteering Karen's services: sometimes I see her doing pro bono work for her friends. Like the time she circumcised our neighbor's baby. The baby was adopted from out of town and came home unexpectedly uncircumcised. Since the baby was not a patient at the local hospital, a simple request to have the baby circumcised led to a whole hospital bureaucratic mess and confusion as to whether an obstetrician or urologist would do the surgery. When the neighbors explained the predicament to Karen, she offered to do it at their house. On the kitchen counter. With their cutlery. You won't see that advertised as one of the many uses for the Ginsu knife. Actually, Karen borrowed the hospital equipment for the procedure, but it was still quite odd. I'm Jewish, so I've seen plenty of circumcisions done in the home. You might think that I wouldn't have found this circum . . . stance unusual. But a circumcision in some-one's home with no bagels and cream cheese anywhere???! Surreal.

A circumcision is at least, or should I say at most, a one-time event. Unlike the recurrent badgering Karen is subject-ed to by friends and relatives seeking birth control pills. This is the most common thing anyone calls for. Especially on the weekend. Men don't realize this, but women, in conjunction with their doctors, have decided, en masse, that they will take their birth control pills so that their period comes during the week, thus leaving their weekend unfettered.

There are some exceptions to this weekend rule. Women will adjust taking their pill to avoid having their period on vacations or on their wedding night, or for a husband's return from a business trip or for when a husband goes away on a business trip. Whatever suits their needs. In general, howev-er, pill packs run out on Saturday.

That means that the weekend is when every on-call OB/GYN in America is pestered by women who want to have sex and just realized that they have no more birth control pills. This is the bane of an OB/GYN's existence. Some doctors instruct their answering service that they will not call in pre-scriptions for birth control pills on the weekend. Others con-tinue to do it and simply curse the patients for not noticing on day 26 that, "Gosh! there are only two more pills in that pack." Karen is of the latter. She figures it's all part of the job. And besides, half the people who call are related.

Call Me Anytime

A little science lesson:

Approximately four weeks after conception a fetus develops an umbilical cord. This becomes a lifeline from mother to baby, providing nourishment and sustenance for the remaining eight months of pregnancy. This you probably knew. What you may not know is that at the same time a second umbilical cord grows from the mother to a little black box hanging from her doctor's belt loop known in Latin as a beeper. This becomes a lifeline from doctor to mother, providing nourishment and sustenance with answers to every single question they have for the remaining eight months of pregnancy.

I despise my wife's beeper. Don't get me wrong: I'm thrilled she's a doctor, but only during office hours. The beeper takes her away from her family, concerts, ballgames and parent-teacher conferences. She missed the entire Iran-Iraq War. On nights when she is on call there is a palpable tension in our house—a sense of dread, waiting for the beeping that will send Karen to the hospital for the night. I try to avoid using the microwave on nights she is on call. It makes her jumpy. When the food is ready the oven emits a beep just like her beeper. You've probably never heard a woman curse a reheated pizza like that. I'm talking before it burns the roof of your mouth.

So as not to seem like a completely selfish ingrate as I complain about my wife's responsibilities, I will tell you that there is one great benefit to her having to take call. While we end up missing events we had hoped to attend, we also have a built-in excuse for not accepting invitations to events we don't want to attend. "Gee, we'd love to go camping and get bitten to death and smell for a few days with you and your four hellions, but darn it if Karen isn't on call that weekend. Make sure you call us again." As a rejection it has more credibility and tact than, "Aww, that's the weekend Karen has to wash her hair."

Now back to my complaints.

The beeper is not the only leash attached to the doctor's collar. There has been one other major technological advancement in modern obstetrical medicine—the cell phone. Now, doctors don't get the luxury of the excuse that they couldn't find a pay phone. For the physician there is no respite.

More than an annoyance, cell phone calls scare me. Especially when Karen is driving. My fear is borne out by the statistic that cell phones are responsible for more driving accidents than drinking. We're going to need new safety campaigns: "Friends don't let friends talk and drive."

It may not be long before you hear this argument in a parking lot:

"Give me the phone, man."

"I'm fine. I know when I've talked enough."

"I'm not letting you get in the car. You're beyond conversational chats, you're dialing random 800 numbers."

"I can handle one short call."

"Only if it's to Talkers Anonymous to get some help."

The beeper and cell phone are the modern doctor's ball and chain. They are so ubiquitous that I wonder how OB/GYNs ever functioned without them. What was it like in the early 1800s? Did they send letters?

Dear Doctor Jaffe,

Just a note to let you know that I broke my water. It's very hot here today, so the wetness was welcome. Wondering what I should do now? Hope this letter finds you well. Looking for-

ward to hearing from you soon.
    Regards,
    Gertrude Smith

I reckon that in the old days (they "reckoned" a lot in the old days), a woman had to ask all her questions in person. I urge Karen to encourage patients to do the same thing. Ask away in the office. Just don't call and interrupt our evening with non-urgent concerns.

First-time mothers are the ones who bring long lists of questions about the safety of every household product on the market to each office visit. They want to know what to eat, how to sleep, maybe they should be breathing differently. It's commendable that they want to do everything right for the health of the baby. Inevitably, in between appointments, something else occurs to them, and Karen will get a call: "Can I paint the nursery?" "Can I fertilize the lawn?" "Can I smoke some crack?" And when the good doctor gives her approval, the next question is invariably, "Will it hurt the baby?" As though it had slipped her mind. Why not just ask the obvious question, "Are you sure you know what you're doing?"

Besides defending my wife's intelligence, I also want to protect her sleep. So, if you're one of Karen's patients, before you call at a ridiculous hour, please think about whether your problem isn't something that can wait until morning. This will come as a surprise to some who do call—doctors are human! In other words, THEY SLEEP! They aren't sauntering about the study at 4:00 AM, pipe in mouth, waiting for your medical emergency. "Why yes, I was anticipating your problem and I've been sitting at my desk for the past four hours going through my old manuals, and I believe I have the solution."

I make this recommendation not just for Karen's or another doctor's sake, but for your own good as well. Really. Would you trust a doctor who came into your exam room with sheet marks on her face, drooling, semi-comatose, saying, " . . . huh?

Huh? What?" Well, that's what you get when you call at 4 a.m.

Obviously, if you are in labor, then the call is necessary. Generally, I only find out that a laboring patient called when I wake up in the morning and find my bedmate missing. Since it isn't my responsibility, I am able to fall back to sleep immediately. I sometimes am in such a deep sleep that I don't even know whether my wife is there or not. One time, I woke up in the morning and congratulated her on getting through the night without so much as a single phone call. She looked at me like I was nuts. She had just gotten back to bed an hour earlier after taking care of a patient from midnight to 6:30.

As a potential middle-of-the-night caller, here's another friendly tip: you should realize that there is the chance that the doctor might already be in the hospital when the answering service calls at home. That means that the doctor's spouse could be the one giving you advice. Morphine is my most frequently prescribed medicine. Just put the lady on a morphine drip and we'll deal with it in the morning. That's the advice I offer either directly to the patient if I pick up the phone, or through Karen when her conversation goes on too long. There are some lengthy calls that do wake me up, and my immediate diagnosis is the one that allows me to go back to sleep. It doesn't matter that I'm not hearing the patient's complaint. I'm awake, it's 4 a.m., and I'm going to keep repeating "morphine drip" until either the patient gets one or I do.

Obviously, I wouldn't make a good doctor. I certainly couldn't manage to be as courteous as Karen is on these calls. Somehow her "caring doctor" phone voice surfaces no matter how cranky she is. Once the wee hour phone call is over, however, I get to hear exactly what she is thinking. "Great! She has a tampon stuck in her. Am I supposed to drive over right now and pull it out?" Over the years, I've learned that these are rhetorical questions, and I'm not supposed to try to answer them.

It's 4 a.m.! Do you know what time it is?

I've encouraged my wife to let her feelings be known when she gets inappropriate phone calls. She never does. That's one of the reasons she's the doctor and I'm a rude plebian. I try to share my emotions. At least when the emotion is annoyance or anger. I'm sure I wouldn't have too many patients, but I'd certainly get a good night's sleep.

I know that *you'd* never call at 4 a.m., but the following are all actual calls received by doctors in the middle of the night. Invariably, the doctors handled themselves professionally and with utmost respect for the patient. All I have changed about these calls is that I have replaced the doctor's given response with what I would have said in the same situation.

PATIENT: I think my pee is coming out the wrong hole.
DOCTOR MARC: If it is, you're probably going to need surgery that is very difficult to do over the phone. More likely, you're drunk.

PATIENT: My yeast infection is bothering me. It started a week ago, but I didn't want to bother you during office hours when doctors are busy, so I thought I'd wait until now.
DOCTOR MARC: You're right, I hate being bothered at my job by job-related questions. If only more people were considerate like you, I could nap during office hours and make up for the sleep I'm not getting now. Why don't you wait until it's stopped bothering you for a week, and then give me a call again.

PATIENT: I've got a terrible headache.

DOCTOR MARC: Take some Tylenol.

PATIENT: Will it hurt the baby?

DOCTOR MARC: Oh, the baby! I forgot about the baby. Here my job is delivering babies, and I completely spaced out about it.

PATIENT: I have a friend who is pregnant and is wondering if she can take aspirin . . . .

DOCTOR MARC: Your friend? Does your friend have a doctor? Do I examine you AND your friends when you come for a checkup? Are your friends covered by your insurance? Is this the 24-hour answer line? Am I just settling a bet? Should I start a radio call-in show?

PATIENT: Doctor, I can't sleep.

DOCTOR MARC: Are you pregnant?

PATIENT: No. My mother died a few days ago, and I'm pretty upset.

DOCTOR MARC: Take some Sominex or other over-the-counter sleeping pill.

(3 nights later, again at 4 a.m.) SAME PATIENT: Hey Doc, you know that stuff you told me to get? . . .

DOCTOR MARC: Yes?

PATIENT: It doesn't work.

PATIENT: I think I'm going to have sex tonight, and I'm out of pills. Can you call in a prescription for me? I don't know what pharmacy is open.

DOCTOR MARC: Well, then I'll just cruise your neighborhood to find out which one is open. Why don't I deliver them for you while I'm at it?

PATIENT: I'm about to have sex . . . .

DOCTOR MARC: I'm like a reverse 976 number. People who

are having sex call me to tell me about it. I should charge $2.99 a minute. Don't they realize that more babies are good for business? I'm probably not the person you should be calling.

PATIENT: I have a bad cold.
DOCTOR MARC: Take some Sudafed.
PATIENT: Will it hurt the baby?
DOCTOR MARC: Only if you inject it into your uterus.

PATIENT: My dog is vomiting—what should I do?
DOCTOR MARC: Excuse me? Your dog? Why don't you call your vet?
PATIENT: At four in the morning? He's sleeping.

PATIENT: Doctor, this is Jan Smith's husband.
DOCTOR MARC: Is there a problem?
PATIENT: Well, I'd like to discuss the bill.
DOCTOR MARC: The bill? At this hour? Go right ahead. I charge $50 an hour for discussing the bill during the day and $50,000 an hour for discussing the bill after midnight, so go right ahead. I've started the clock.

PATIENT: I have crabs.
DOCTOR MARC: Well, you'll have to get this medicine tomorrow.
PATIENT: I'm desperate. I need it now.
DOCTOR MARC: There's an all-night pharmacy at the corner of Main and Central.
PATIENT: What's their number?
DOCTOR MARC: I don't know.
PATIENT: Why not?
DOCTOR MARC: Because I'm not 411.

PATIENT: Can I use nail polish remover?

DOCTOR MARC: I don't care.
PATIENT: Will it hurt the baby?
DOCTOR MARC: If you drink it.

PATIENT: Doc, I'm in terrible pain.
DOCTOR MARC: Fine. I'll meet you at the hospital . . .
PATIENT: Oh. It's not that bad.
DOCTOR MARC: So it's not bad enough that it needs to be treated, it's just bad enough that you need to wake me.

PATIENT: My contractions are not very strong and only coming every half hour . . .
DOCTOR MARC: You don't need to go to the hospital yet.
PATIENT: I knew I wasn't ready to go in. What I really wanted to know is if you think now is a good time to take a shower.
DOCTOR MARC: Sure. Go soak your head.

PATIENT: I haven't been getting along with my family. Do you think we should sell the house?
DOCTOR MARC: You seem to be confusing doctor and realtor, which I can understand, because they are probably listed next to each other in your phone book.

PATIENT: I can't sleep on my left side anymore.
DOCTOR MARC: So roll over.
PATIENT: Will it hurt the baby?
DOCTOR MARC: If you fall off the bed when you do it.

PATIENT: I have a cough.
DOCTOR MARC: Take some cough drops.
PATIENT: Will it hurt the baby?
DOCTOR MARC: There is a chance your baby will look like the Smith Brothers.

PATIENT: I'm really embarrassed, but the dog ate my pessary.

DOCTOR MARC: He can't eat homework like a normal dog?

PATIENT: The condom just broke. What should I do?
DOCTOR MARC: Pray? Oh, and maybe you can get a refund.

PATIENT: The condom just broke. Can I get a morning-after pill?
DOCTOR MARC: I guess. What pharmacy should I call?
PATIENT: I don't know a pharmacy around here.
DOCTOR MARC: Where are you?
PATIENT: I'm at a phone booth in Las Vegas.
DOCTOR MARC: Well, do you feel lucky?

PATIENT: The condom broke. I need the morning-after pill.
DOCTOR MARC: Do you know why it's called the morning-after pill?
PATIENT: Because you take it the morning after?
DOCTOR MARC: Bingo! It's the single most appropriately named drug. So don't call me till the morning!

Don't I Know You?

The invasion of my wife's work into our private life doesn't end at the telephone receiver. Doctors are minor celebrities at any social gathering. It's cliché for people to meet a doctor at a party and start asking about their medical problems. I now know how it became cliché. Everyone does it. The most amazing thing isn't that they do it, it's the degree to which women will reveal deeply personal things while I'm standing right there next to Karen. IUDs, cramping, sore breasts, plans for getting a labial ring, you name it, women are seeking free and immediate counsel. If it's a dull party, I suggest that they lie on a nearby couch and have the doctor give them an exam right there.

As incredible as that openness may seem, it is even more amazing to me that when Karen is introduced, nearly every woman recognizes her name as someone who is an obstetrician/gynecologist in the community. We're talking about a greater metropolitan population of about two million, of which, let's say, a third are adult females, and they ALL know her. How?

Apparently women are much more involved and concerned about medical care than men. They research doctors, talk to one another about their doctors, even regularly see their doctors. Unless there is some major medical problem, men have no contact with a doctor. If we need a doctor, we can find one in the yellow pages. If one doctor had a discount coupon, we'd base our decision on that as much as anything else. Women, even if they don't know them, would recognize the name of every doctor in the city. Me, and I speak for all men here, I can name two doctors: My own and Dr. Kevorkian. That's it.

Men don't discuss doctors, because we don't sit around discussing our health very much. We may discuss athletic achievements, but not our health. Women confide in each other, learn from each other, become informed about their bodies and, by extension, their doctors. Men avoid doctors and avoid discussing medical issues with friends. That is doubly true when it comes to our reproductive organs. It takes a plague of extreme trouble to get us to talk to a friend about whether we should even see a doctor. Like, your penis falls off. Even then, the subject would be broached as a third-party incident. A very close friend might say to his buddy, "Have you ever heard of anyone's penis falling off? Do you think that's something to go see a doctor about?"

Even when men are regular visitors they don't bond with their doctors the way women do. Karen has one patient who has become a friend, and she schedules her annual appointment just before lunch so they can go out together afterward. "Let's do a Pap and lunch." she says. A man would have trouble going out for a meal with his doctor after his annual prostate exam. We have a hard time separating the person from the event that just occurred. Conversation would be strained. A likely lunch conversation would go like this:

DOC: Sure is hot out.
PATIENT: I just had this horrible realization that five minutes ago you had your finger up my ass.
DOC: Yep. I'm going to have the corned beef sandwich, how about you?
PATIENT: Eat?! How can you eat with those hands that just had your finger up my ass!
DOC: Let's get your mind off of this. So what's wrong with the Dodgers? Think they'll fire Davey Johnson?
PATIENT: No doubt. They're losing and he manages like . . .

he's got a finger up his ass! I'm sorry. I have to leave.

Of course, not all gynecologists get close to their patients. Probably any attempts by a male gynecologist to establish a social relationship with a patient would be taboo. The most awkward situation would be when a relationship exists prior to the doctor/patient relationship. Consider the resident I met who was dreading entering private practice. His mother had told him she couldn't wait until he was a doctor because she wanted to send all her friends to him. Yuch! I know I couldn't deal with that. The thought gives me chills. It's not just the discomfort of the situation, it's the awkwardness of not knowing what to call them. Is it Mrs. Kennebrew or simply Erma? And if I call her Erma, will she quit telling my assistants about the time I peed in her flower garden? One thing I know, that resident won't be going back to the old neighborhood block party.

Yet a woman gynecologist can establish a relationship with their patient outside the office. Some of Karen's best friends are patients whose babies she has delivered. There is an intimacy that can develop when you are bringing someone's child into the world. But it doesn't happen with all her patients. There are plenty whom Karen doesn't feel friendly with. There are many whom she wouldn't even recognize as patients if she saw them walking down the street.

Karen requests that if you are a patient of hers, and you run into her outside of the office, please introduce yourself as such. She has something like 30,000 patients and can't possibly remember every one. It will drive her crazy if she thinks she knows you, but she's not sure from where. And she'll have to call you "You," as in "Good to see YOU . . . how are YOU . . . Oh YOU old YOU YOU." What she really wants to know is, "Who the hell are YOU?"

Karen promotes her own trouble in this regard. She has the unique gift of being able to make each patient feel like a personal friend. During an annual office visit she will remember your birthday, and she never fails to inquire about Aunt Jenny or your recent trip to Jamaica. You are shocked that your doctor would recall an intimate, private detail and therefore feel like Karen really cares. Ladies, it's a parlor trick. It's in your chart. If you mention that your husband got a new job, Karen doesn't remember that a year later. Hell, she doesn't remember when *I* get a new job. She simply jots down a note in your chart and then, a year later, references it before walking into the room. You are amazed that she cared enough to remember, and now consider her a close friend. It's great for business. However, it's terrible when she meets the same patient in public and can't recall her name, let alone hubby's profession.

(The other little parlor trick Karen has is her ability to draw upside down. This is a useful skill in trying to explain a procedure to a patient. While facing the patient, she will scribble a beautifully proportioned schematic of the operation she hopes to perform. The patient looks on in awe, probably not understanding the medical procedure, but gaining complete confidence that anyone who can draw upside down like that can surely pull out a uterus.)

Sometimes, when she sees a patient in public, Karen will try to use me in a ploy to get her name. "Here's the plan," she will whisper conspiratorially. "You go over and introduce yourself, she'll say her name, and then I'll come over and you introduce us before I do the phony 'of course, I know you' routine." Not a bad plan if I were James Bond. Then I would be good at introducing myself. I would know my line. But I'm not very socially adept. Conjuring up the grace it takes to start a conversation with a stranger at a party leaves me too drained to remember someone's name just seconds after I've heard it. By the time Karen comes over I've forgotten it, the ruse is a failure, and we are both embarrassed. Later Karen pulls me to a remote corner of the party and slaps me silly.

If you want to give other identifying information when you meet your doctor on the street, that is perfectly acceptable, although one should be discreet. Names and ages of children the doctor delivered are welcome. Yelling across an aisle of a crowded grocery store, "Doctor! Doctor, you cured my gonorrhea!" is not. That actually happened to a colleague of Karen's. Just one more reason to wash your produce.

People do trap their doctors in the oddest places. Another of Karen's contemporaries was driving to the health club early one Sunday morning. She was stopped at a light when she heard a tapping on her window. She turned to see a woman who was frantic about something. Flat tire? Stalled car? A horrible accident? The doctor rolled down her window. "Doctor, I leak urine when I orgasm." she complained. Oh, so this was a patient, and here was a problem that needed emergency medical roadside assistance. "Gosh," replied the quick-thinking doc, "Why don't you lie down in the back seat and I'll examine you. We'll have to hurry, because the light is about to change."

So I'm just saying, when your doctor sees you out of context, it may be hard to place you. Plus, your doctor is used to seeing you in a different position. The look of confusion on your doctor's face is because she didn't realize you were so tall. So perhaps you shouldn't bother with names or giving your medical history. If you meet your gynecologist outside the office and you want her to recognize you, you should find the nearest table and lie down.

Office Hours

Karen and I have very different work styles. Much of that is a result of our completely different jobs. Some of it is personality-based. I am generally relaxed and scattershot, while she is focused and directed. Karen is on a schedule from the moment she wakes up. She needs to be in the office by 9 because every 15 minutes another patient or two come in. If she falls behind early she'll have to skip lunch. Meanwhile, I should be at my desk by 9 because every 15 minutes or so another sentence comes along. If I don't have a paragraph written by noon, then . . . hey, it's lunch! This book took me 112 years to write.

The clock rules Karen's life. So many patients, so little time. The time crunch manifests itself every morning. She is a maniac trying to get out of the house. Some days she has the added burden of taking the kids to school. Those mornings there is lots of pushing, cajoling and yelling. I try to help, but we have three girls ages 8, 6, and 4, and I don't understand this whole concept of shoes. Why do they need to be a part of the whole ensemble? Don't tennis shoes go with everything? At some point in fetal development, the brains of girl babies and boy babies diverge. As babies they hear the same thing, but begin to interpret the words differently. Shoes are the classic example. Infant girls and boys are told the following sentence: "You need one pair of shoes for every outfit." Girl babies will process that sentence so that beginning at age five, girls will feel compelled to purchase one pair of shoes for each and every outfit. Boy babies will interpret that sentence to mean that they need one pair of shoes that will cover every possible outfit. Some kind of formal tennis shoe with a steel toe and we'd be all set. I know raising boys has its unique problems. Figuring out which pair of shoes to wear each morning isn't one of them.

Instead of helping the kids get dressed, I concentrate on breakfast. Breakfast could be pancakes with fresh strawberries or a cheese omelet and some raisin toast. It could be, if the kids would get ready. Instead, I serve Nutri-Grain bars. Don't think this doesn't require some skill. If the bar is injured or deformed in any way in the unwrapping process it can cause an emotional display that includes a reprise of scenes from *The Exorcist*. Believe me, I've become an expert Nutri-Grain bar unwrapperer.

All this rushing in the morning is a courtesy to Karen's patients. She doesn't want to make them wait. That promptness is tricky to maintain throughout the day, as patients can easily lose track of the time when discussing their own health. Karen does her best to keep to her appointment schedule while still being nice and not making it seem like the patient is being moved along an assembly line. Being a doctor is the opposite of being a talk-show host. You aren't looking for those charming anecdotes or the interesting story about how you danced for the Queen of England. The short answers work well here. Karen avoids open-ended questions. If a patient is there for pelvic pain, a "How are you feeling?" could elicit a long-winded self-diagnosis that suggests it all started with a trauma from a dodge ball game in the fourth grade. That's irrelevant and redundant. Every physical and emotional problem any of us has can be traced back to a dodge ball game in the fourth grade. That's already in your chart. Tell the doctor something she doesn't know.

Dr. Jaffe faces the challenge of extracting the pertinent information concisely and with charm. She will say something like, "Glad to hear you're in good health other than your pelvic pain. What's the one word that would best describe the pain?" Notice how in two sentences she not only encourages her patient to be succinct, she also discourages her from talking about any other problems.

That is a quirk of mine that she has warned me is not appreciated by the doctor. I don't go to see a doctor unless I am certain something is wrong. However, once I'm already at the doctor's, even if it's for, say, chest pains, I figure, "Hey, I'm here . . . might as well ask him about my sore wrist and that fungal toenail." Karen tells me that doctors don't like when a patient does that. I think it's helpful to consolidate.

Having hustled through a morning of patients, Karen will have a desk full of charts to get through and phone calls to return. She is able to efficiently dispatch with these, except when she gets that daily nuisance phone call. I know I'm probably disturbing her, but I can't help myself. The phone is right there and I get bored eating my chocolates, watching my soaps, and concocting excuses as to why I'm not going to have dinner on the table. So I'll call just to chat about some insignificant thing like a small kitchen fire or our daughter's broken arm, and she quickly dispatches me with a gruff report that I'm disturbing her patient flow. I can't help but picture the scene on the other end: Karen is sitting there with a patient in her office and the yell comes from the staff, "Dr. Jaffe, your husband on line one." She says excuse me, gives a few curt "Yes dears" into the receiver, hangs up the phone and with a snide chuckle turns to the patient and says, "The old ball and chain." Then she picks up her cigar, puts her feet back up on her desk and says, "Now where we? . . . Your pelvic pain, yes . . . ."

Keeping her doctorly, reassuring demeanor in a frenetic, intense atmosphere is a special skill. Karen gets into a rhythm. A groove. My calls probably mess up that rhythm. She's thinking cervixes, and I'm calling about cerviche. (O.K., I don't typically make cerviche, but allow me some poetic license.) I'm a bother. At least until she gets home. Then, she wonders why I didn't remind her she has to leave in five minutes for "Mommy's night" at preschool.

Usually there is some event to attend to when she gets home. With three kids it's almost impossible to relax. Karen tries to be the breadwinner and the perfect mom. She succeeds more often than she fails. It's rare that she misses any important events. Patients often tell her that they are amazed that she does what she does while raising three kids. She graciously credits her husband for making it all possible, but kids need their mom, and Karen is there when needed. Unlike a colleague of hers, who sent one of the office staff to a school event in her stead. Andrea was a filing assistant, so it was easier for her than the doctor to leave the busy office. Since Andrea had never met the physician's children, she gave Andrea pictures of them so she would know whom to be proud of when their part in the school presentation came up. It wasn't hard for the kids to recognize Andrea. The 27-year-old stood out on what happened to be Grandparents' Day.

Given all her responsibilities of motherhood and doctordom, Karen relishes her free time. Her concept of resting is, oddly enough, resting. She likes to sleep. She likes to nap. She likes to recline. My idea of relaxation is different. I like to run, go, do. I sit at a desk all day. In my house. When I get a break I want to get up, get out and see the world. She wants to see the bed.

Vacations are problematic because of this. We need someplace interesting and challenging that also has a comfortable chaise lounge. Our ideal place would be somewhere on the Gulf. As in The Persian Gulf. Iraq, for example. Karen could lie on the beach while I go trolling through Basra looking for chemical weapons. I'm surprised they don't have package tours.

Lord knows what this means for our dessert days. (Dessert days come well after the salad days. And if you live right, it comes after the main course days, and still well before the "I'll take the check" days.) I'm looking at retirement as an opportunity to learn and travel. If we could save enough money, living in a place like Europe or the Middle East for a few years holds appeal. Karen will want to spend it on a Caribbean island, which would drive me coconuts. So what will we do? I have a solution. When we hit 65, I'm going to med school. Karen will train to become a writer. For her that means a lot of reading and nodding off. We both can't wait.

Handywoman

My wife is very handy around the house. You would expect that, given her surgical skills, she would be good with her hands. You would think that she would be especially good with fine motor skills, like repairing the dishwasher or cutting the grass—those being two of our finer motors. She can't. She complains that she has no hand-eye coordination. That's not exactly what you'd like to hear from someone who is wielding a laser in an attempt to remove your uterus, so Karen doesn't tell that to her patients.

Let me ease her patients' fears, however. Karen will explain that she has no hand-eye coordination when there is a large object in her hand, like a tennis racket or a golf club. That's why she doesn't play tennis or golf. However, with a small instrument like a scalpel or a laser she is very skilled. Makes sense to me. But a doctor who doesn't golf? That gives pause.

So given that her skills are limited to surgical tools, how is she handy around the house? She's always ready with a tape measure. I never have to look for one, I just ask Karen and she's got it on her. OBs use a tape measure to measure pregnant girth and fetal growth, which, I gather from the fact that Karen always has her tape measure with her, happens constantly. I could wake her up in the middle of the night, "Honey, I need to measure the living room." Bingo! She'd whip her roll right out of some secret pocket in her pajamas. She is never without it. I suspect that she's measuring non-pregnant women too. She could be doubling as a tailor for all I know. "Your baby seems to be growing fine. Make an appointment for six weeks from now and I'll have these pants hemmed by Friday." She can do a digital exam and get your inseam at the same time. I don't know how she does it.

The other item that an OB will always have with her is her little due date wheel. You come in, tell your doctor when your last period was, and she spins the wheel and tells you when the baby is due. It seems to me that going to the obstetrician is very similar to one of those games on the midway. You pay your money and spin the wheel. The doctor guesses your baby's birth date and, by using a tape measure, guesses the baby's birth weight. I think if the doctor is off by a week or more than a pound, you should be able to pick a giant stuffed animal from the top shelf.

Perks

I remember, many years ago, being unable to get last-minute reservations at a snazzy restaurant. A friend advised me to say I was a doctor, suggesting that prefix would give me immediate access to the establishment's forbidden fruits and vegetables and beef tenderloins. I had heard that before so I tried it. No luck. Even back then, being a doctor didn't carry the weight it once did. I wondered why doctors ever held sway in that manner. Did the restaurateur figure that the doctor would reciprocate one day and let him into the hospital when it's booked? "I apologize, sir, but we have no space in the hospital. You can't expect a last-minute bed on a Saturday night . . . I'm sorry you're having a heart attack, but there truly is no . . . wait a minute . . . you're the guy who owns Chez Oo La La! Come on, I'll get you in." Maybe they used to think it would be good to have a doctor around to do the Heimlich on choking patrons. Once those laminated charts came out and waiters became schooled in the Heimlich maneuver, the doctor's perk disappeared. Now saying you're a doctor doesn't get you in anywhere.

It can get you out of things. Speeding tickets, to be specific. It works for Karen. She plays a little game with herself to see how fast she can get between home and the hospital on a 3 a.m. run to deliver a baby. She can't seem to break the four-minute barrier. She almost did once, but a cop stopped her. He asked where she was going in such a hurry at 3 a.m. on a weeknight. She told him she was on her way home from delivering a baby, and the cop just waved her on. She made it in four minutes, thirty-six seconds.

If you are going to use the "I'm a doctor" excuse, it helps to have scrubs on. That makes you look more official. You might want to carry a set in your car for a quick change when necessary. And, if the police officer is persistent and asks questions, I would advise saying your specialty is obstetrics rather than, say, dermatology. It's much harder to convince law enforcement that there is an acne emergency that needs immediate attention.

One expected perk of being married to a doctor is receiving great medical care. It's a misconception. First of all, Karen is not my doctor. Most of my problems are orthopedic-type troubles, and Karen can't stomach anything to do with the musculoskeletal parts of the body. Just the thought of me cracking my neck gives her the willies (medical term for the heebie-jeebies).

So I have to go to a doctor, just like anybody else.

In this age of insurance, professional courtesy is rarely given, and I certainly don't get any special medical treatments just because my wife is a colleague. There are no secret medicines that doctors save for their best patients. Nothing like the following conversation has ever taken place:

MY INTERNIST: Marc, your cholesterol is a little high, and I don't do this for most patients, but since you're Karen's husband, here, take this.

ME: A gummi bear?

INTERNIST: Yep. Hard to believe, but a pack of these a day and your cholesterol will be right where it should be. Many years ago we realized that kids don't have cholesterol problems and we put two and two together and . . . well, again, it's just because you're Karen's husband . . . Don't go tell anyone, or it would put us out of business.

The advantage I have comes when I get home from a doctor's visit and Karen can explain to me what is happening. She can reassure me that my doctor is doing the right thing:

ME: What's this pill do?
KAREN: It will make you feel better.
ME: He said to take one per rectum. Do I have more than one rectum?
KAREN: 'Per' means 'in'.
ME: Awww! Do I have to?
KAREN: What? Did you think you'd get special treatment?
ME: Yes.
KAREN: Well, it is in the shape of a gummi bear.

The sole courtesy I am afforded by virtue of my marriage is physician accessibility. While for the general public, getting your name onto certain doctors' schedules can be as difficult as getting your name on Steven Spielberg's day runner, if I need to be seen, I will get seen in a timely manner.

Let me assure you that my butting in is not to the reason the average person is unable to get a doctor's appointment until some time in the messianic era. It isn't the doctor's fault either. It's the receptionist. The person who answers the phone and does the schedule. Courtesy cases like myself excluded, doctors don't decide who is on their schedule. The receptionist does. Doctors just ask to be pointed to a room with a patient. It's the receptionist that decides who is in there. Get by the receptionist and you're golden. That is no easy task, however.

Physicians' receptionists are trained to stop you. They all get their schooling at the same top-secret facility located underground somewhere in the Mojave desert. They are given specific instructions to never book anyone before their condition will have improved on its own. Their attitude is—pregnancy is over after nine months, you can see the doctor in ten. Their credo is—illness, like life, is only temporary, we'll get to you when it ends. Their religion—surely, they're all Christian Scientists.

Not only do I get seen quickly, but I get seen by the right doctors. I have an insider's knowledge of which doctors are the good doctors. I hear stories about the ones that aren't. I'm also told how to be a good patient. I hear stories about the patients that aren't. I hear lots of stories. Dinner conversations in our house are often intimate, they just happen to be other people's intimacies. They are sometimes funny, sometimes sad, and sometimes simply unbelievable. Traditionally, Karen tells her stories after the kids have left the table and I'm clearing. That way we don't face the difficulty of explaining things to the kids and, if the story is good enough, I've been so rapt that I've washed the dishes and cleaned the kitchen before realizing it was Karen's turn to do so.

I'm guessing that being married to a doctor is probably the same as being married to anyone else, only with better stories. I share those stories with you here because we simply don't have enough chairs to invite you all over for dinner.

Excuse the kids from the table before you tell them.

A DAY AT THE OFFICE

Behind Exam Room Doors

They Only Serve Those Who Wait

A doctor's office is divided into two separate time/space dimensions. For the doctor and the office staff, everything is moving very fast. There is not enough time in the day. The patients are being seen in rapid succession. Meanwhile, the patients' world moves at a very slow pace. There is time to read magazines, file nails and do your taxes before the doctor actually sees you. The only place in a doctor's office that moves at the same speed for both patient and doctor is the elevator going up to the office. Federal regulations require all medical building elevators to move at the rate of two feet per millennium.

It's very important to Karen to keep to her daily schedule. She hates running late and assumes it bothers patients to sit around waiting. She is, I believe, unique in this regard. Most doctors inevitably run behind. That's why they have waiting rooms. That's not to say that time spent there is completely wasted. There are forms that generally need to be filled out. New patients will have to fill out the "new patient form" with insurance information. Returning patients don't have to bother with that. They can simply fill out the "We're making sure we have the updated information on your insurance form" which looks strangely the same as the new patient form. Newly pregnant patients have extra forms about their family history and health. One typical form asks questions like:

How old will you be when the baby is born?

How old will the baby's father be?

How old will the baby be? (Trick question just to see if you understand the whole concept.)

Do you smoke?

How much?

Of course if you answered "No" to "Do you smoke?" you don't have to answer the "How much?" question. Or you could put down any number. "I don't smoke two packs a day. Hell, 100 packs! I am like a closed chimney, I'm constantly not smoking."

Once you are done with the forms and hand them back to the women who are having some kind of party behind the sliding, frosted-glass windows, it's time for the first part of your wait. For women at the OB/GYN's, I figure this isn't so bad. The waiting room is full of other women to talk to. There are lots of magazines to read. As with most doctors offices, OB's have subject appropriate magazines like: *Women's Health, Working Mother, BabyCare, Women's Mothers, Working Baby*, or some combination of the above. With so much to read and do, women find the time in the waiting room goes by relatively quickly.

Men who accompany their wives to the gynecologist feel the waiting room is some kind of interminable purgatory. The magazines are of absolutely no interest to the men. There's no one for us to talk to. All men can do is count the number of people in the waiting room and try to calculate how long a wait it's going to be. That, or play the "I wonder what she's here for?" game, which you can only win if you go up to a stranger and ask them. Even if they tell you and you are right, your wife shoots you for being such a cad and you die, so you lose anyway. So generally, men use this downtime to take a nap. Properly embarrassed by the man snoring or drooling next to them, the wife moves away, and that explains why each OB's office has an unclaimed man sleeping in the corner.

Once your name is called, the real wait comes. Doctor's offices work like Disneyland. They try to keep you moving so your line doesn't seem so long. They do this by having a short line out front without telling you that it's really just a line to get in the big line in back. For the doctor, the big line in back is the exam room.

You better hope you've carried a magazine in there with you, because once they close the exam room door there is no going back. There is never anything to read in that little room. Actually there are the diplomas on the wall. That's why diplomas are in Latin. You'll have enough time to teach yourself a new language.

Or figure out how to put on the gown.

If you go to a doctor with an especially helpful staff, you might find the gown laid out for you as if your mother came in while you were in the waiting room and picked it out for you. This is unlikely. Chances are it is folded and very confusing. There are no tags to figure out which end is the back. In fact, you can't always distinguish between the top and the bottom and, adding to the danger, it is one of the few articles of clothing that you will ever wear that could potentially give you a paper cut.

The gowns also come in one-size-fits-all. That is a lie. One full-figured woman must have decided that it worked best as an ersatz skirt. The doctor finally came in to find her with her bottom barely covered and her top completely exposed.

It would have been the perfect time to tell the doctor something that we all would probably like to say to a doctor once in our lives. "I'm not quite ready. Why don't you go sit in your office with a magazine and I'll be in shortly."

Making Babies

Cultural wisdom holds that if you really want something and are willing to work hard at it and have patience, then you will eventually get what you want. This wisdom has nothing to do with getting pregnant. Just witness the appointment schedule in any OB's office. It will always include a woman who didn't want to be pregnant and is. It also will likely include at least one woman who wants to be and isn't. In fact, scientists have found the following hierarchy of women, arranged in order from most likely to least likely to get pregnant in any given sexual encounter:

1) Single women who aren't in a relationship
2) Single women with a boyfriend who will bolt the second he finds out she's pregnant
3) Married women who don't want kids
4) Married women whose husbands have had a vasectomy
5) Virgins
6) Married women trying to have kids

Then there are those rare women that get pregnant just by looking at a guy. At least they say that's how it happened. "But Mom, Dad, I just looked at him." We know that in truth looking at a boy doesn't get you pregnant. It's when you close your eyes for a second that does it. Especially if the last time you did look, both of you were naked.

The ease with which some can get pregnant is infuriating to those who fall into category six. If you are married and trying to have kids, don't despair. There is still a much greater chance that you will conceive than not. For those who do have trouble at first, well, hard work and patience are things you will need. Trying hard doesn't mean hanging upside down for an hour after intercourse to let gravity help sperm get to egg, though you're welcome to try that. Some women have been known to lie on their back, put their legs in the air and bicycle pump to get that sperm down. Or up, as the case may be. They are wasting their time. The womb is like space. It's all floating around in there, and sperm can float right past the egg. You could have sex on a gyroscope in the anti-gravity lab at NASA and it wouldn't affect your chances of getting pregnant. It could hurt your chances of becoming an astronaut . . . or increase them, depending on who the sex was with, but medical science doesn't delve into those matters.

Trying hard does mean checking your temperature to determine your ovulation time and having a husband able to perform under pressure. There are some men who have trouble with that. Others rise to the occasion, so to speak. None, I dare say, have risen to the occasion more than a young couple who were taking to the challenge of conception with particular gusto.

They had come into the OB's office upset that they had not gotten pregnant on the first try. The doctor assured them that this was not unusual, but asked about the couple's approach. The woman explained that she had figured out her approximate ovulation time and they would set the peak day aside for lovemaking. Some people set aside an hour, others a few minutes, but these two were still young and in love and anxious to conceive. They had sex twelve times in 12 hours! They figured the more sperm that was in there, the better their chances were. What they didn't understand is that although men can ejaculate often in a 24-hour period, it is only the first two times that carry really active sperm. So twelve times in 12 hours was a bit of overkill. I must say, however, that I, and I think everyone reading this, applaud their determination.

Men generally have a hangup that equates virility with the ability to father children. If they can get it up, they figure it's a guarantee that they can father children, and assume that any trouble must be the woman's. In fact, over 40% of infertility problems are related to the man. While it's simple for the man to be checked for infertility problems, there are many who beg off when asked to jerk off. Like it's an affront to their masculinity to masturbate. Did these guys completely skip high school? Most men have trained their whole lives for this occasion. Many have wondered whether masturbation could be a career option. Yet, let the world know where and when it's happening, and they become shy.

Testing is done in the andrology lab, or the "collection" room. That's a euphemism that doesn't fool anybody. The locals call it the "masturbatorium." The considerate hospitals try to put it in a discreet spot. A discreet location helps comfort the patient. In other words it's good for the test ease. (Don't complain! I've got more bad puns like that and I'm not afraid to use them.) The problem is that when it's tucked away in a remote corner of the hospital, the patients have to ask how to get there. The receptionist must have a hard time concealing a little wink and smile every time a man asks for directions. Even if the receptionist is named Vito. The alternative is to post cutesy hospital signs saying, "To the masturbatorium" with a penis pointing the direction down the hall.

Inside, the rooms should be nice and clean with a reasonable choice of stimulants. Some have X-rated videos. The ones that haven't been updated in a while have *National Geographics* and old Farrah Fawcett posters on the wall. No experience could have been worse than that of the man who had to deliver while the "collection" room was accidentally locked and inaccessible. His only option was to go into an unused janitor's closet while the nurse guarded the door. His sole stimulus was the Virginia Slims ad on the back of a Time magazine.

The men who object to donating their fluids are generally the same guys who, in a different stage of life, would cringe if asked to have a vasectomy. The most common statement men make is, "Nobody, but nobody is cutting anywhere near there." Despite medical proof and doctors' reassurances that a vasectomy doesn't affect sexual function, men still relate the two. It's all psychological. Men are afraid of losing their vigor and an inability to father a child somehow makes us older. In the back of our minds we are all still 18. That's when men reach their sexual peak. Men should realize, however, that 18 is just a physical peak, and that with the proper attitude and perspective, they can enhance their sex life beyond what it was then. With or without a vasectomy, your sex life can keep improving as you age. I feel mine has. Why, when I was 18 I would go all night to satisfy a woman. Now, one time, and my wife is satisfied for a month. So you see, I'm getting better at it. I'll bet Mr. 12-times-in-12-hours is envious.

In order to help bashful men part with a sample of their sperm, some doctors allow their patients to collect it at home. This is possible only when the sperm can be brought into the lab within an hour. And it needs to be kept warm during that hour. Patients are told to wrap the container in a warm towel, or better yet, keep the sperm close to their body. Under the armpit is a good place. That's where one woman was keeping her husband's sample as she sped to the lab. Why she was taking it and not him, I'm not certain. I'm sure, somewhere in the argument over who was bringing it he said, "Look, normally after sex you're carrying the sperm, so . . . ." Whatever he said, it worked, and here she was, driving to the hospital, one arm on the wheel, the other squeezing her precious cargo under her armpit. Under normal driving conditions the hospital was an hour and five minutes away, so she was going a bit over the speed limit. Yes, she was stopped for speeding.

The cop sauntered up to the car, unaware that the woman was becoming frantic over her shipment. He barely had a chance to say, "Howdy, ma'am," when she screamed at him, "My sperm! My sperm!" and then reached under her jacket to show him her valuable container. Officers of the law are cautious of anyone reaching near their arm, as it is a place for a shoulder holster and a concealed weapon. He instantly pulled his gun and yelled "Freeze!" In a matter of seconds, she was spread-eagle up against the car. When she was finally able to explain her predicament, she was given a police escort. Her husband should have felt proud. Not many guys get a police escort. Even fewer have their sperm get a police escort.

Another woman took a different approach to keeping her husband's sperm warm. It arrived at the hospital, and the lab technician was able to tell that there was something seriously wrong with her husband's reproductive capability. The semen was all clumped together. It was clearly abnormal. He asked the woman if it was kept warm in transit. She said that in order to be certain that it stayed warm, she had microwaved it for five minutes before driving over. Medically, it didn't matter whether she had used the "Reheat" or "Beverage" setting. The sperm was fried.

Clumping is not one of the more traditional problems that men have with their sperm. If there is something wrong it's usually that there isn't any sperm. Or too few. Or that the sperm has no tails or no heads. Or that they just swim in circles like one-armed drunks. These are known as dizzy sperm. Whatever the problem, you can be certain that it will require more tests. Tests like the "Hamster Penetration Test." (Personally, that's where I would put my foot down and refuse to submit myself to any more tests.) It's not quite what it sounds. They take the sperm and see if it can penetrate a hamster egg. This is just to know whether the sperm's problem is that it's not finding the egg or not peeling the egg when it finds it. Don't worry. Those that do get through don't form some sort of weird half hamster, half human. I'll leave it to you to write your own sci-fi horror about a secret lab where very strange, hairy humans with pink eyes run on giant hamster wheels.

These tests are traumatic for many infertile couples. Struggling as they are with their inability to conceive, they have the additional humiliation of having their romance reduced to chemistry. Everyone knows why we have babies. No one seems to know why we don't have them when we should. And the tests go on. If it's not the man, it's most likely the woman. Then, finding the problem can be tougher. Although not in all cases.

One woman was concerned about her inability to conceive. She had been trying for six months with no success. Although doctors don't officially consider it an infertility "problem" until a couple has tried for a full year, six months can seem like an eternity to a couple anxious for children. Her doctor listened to her plight and then took the first step toward solving the problem; she examined her. The examination revealed that the woman had her diaphragm in. The patient said she had wondered where she put it. The next month she was pregnant. Another infertility problem solved! Investigative gynecology at its finest.

Even more miraculous was the couple who had been trying for two years with no success. They were from the Dominican Republic and had seen all the doctors down there. They had heard of a specialist in the States and were able to make arrangements to come see the great doctor Houdini. (Not his real name.) All their records were shipped from the Dominican Republic, and it looked like it would be difficult to determine quickly why such a young couple, in their early 20s, was infertile. Houdini decided to open with a post-coital test.

The post-coital test is where a couple has intercourse at home, and then rushes immediately to the hospital so the doctor can check the woman's vagina and see whether the man's sperm is enjoying its new digs. If the sperm is doing fine, they move on to other tests. If the sperm is acting like the vagina is Mars and they don't have their space suit on, well, then, you've got your problem right there. At least with the post-coital, you get to have intercourse at home and not in a little hospital room called the "screwatorium."

This couple failed miserably in the post-coital test. It's not like they found only a few live sperm, limping, wounded, but hopelessly determined. There was no sperm. None! The test needed to be repeated. It was, and with the same result—no sperm. This was very puzzling even for the great Houdini. So he asked them a few questions about how they were having intercourse. Was there penetration? Yes, was the answer. Was there premature ejaculation? No. "O.K.," said a confused Houdini, "just describe how you had intercourse." The couple proceeded to describe anal intercourse as they had been doing it since their honeymoon.

A month later they were pregnant. The couple was happy to pay Houdini's full bill. If only so he wouldn't tell anybody.

Could You Please Pass the . . . Eww!

My sex life is full of tales of illicit behavior and deviant practice. My sex life itself has no illicit behavior and deviant practice, just *tales* about those activities. Karen will tell me about some patient's sexual activity, and then I'll ask if we could do that. Karen usually reminds me that a) we are normal, and that b) I complain about the electric bill as it is.

That's O.K. As I've grown older and had kids, my fantasies have changed. It's to the point now where I'll see a beautiful 19-year-old and I'll think, "I'll bet that if I approached her . . . used some of my better lines . . . she would be willing . . . to babysit."

If Karen is telling me about some odd sexual practice, chances are that whatever the behavior is, it has led to a medical problem. I'm surprised sometimes because I thought that by now everyone knows about "safe sex." Not just condoms, but the preponderance of opportunities for satisfaction without any real contact. There's phone sex, cybersex, and so forth. My understanding of the definition of premature orgasm now is—"an orgasm which occurs before you've even typed in your credit card number."

Despite what I thought, people like Viv find new ways of practicing unsafe sex.

Viv came into the office somewhat distraught over the fact that she had a sexually transmitted disease. She had assumed it meant that her husband had had an affair, because she had not been with anyone else. Viv was upset and confused. She felt they had a fulfilling sex life. She said she always kept things interesting by bringing home sex toys that she would get at sex-toy parties.

"Sex-toy parties?" Karen asked.

"Yes" responded Viv, eager to tell all about her monthly gathering. "It's kind of like a Tupperware party. A woman is the distributor, and she invites a group of ladies over for lunch and we all try out sex toys and decide what we like."

"And do you use a condom on these sex toys?" inquired Karen.

A suspicious "No" was the answer. "But I don't think those toys are realistic enough to get you pregnant."

"Well, no . . ." continued Karen, "But you clean Tupperware before you use it, don't you?"

It finally hit Viv that she had contracted this disease from a hand-me-down sex toy. Take this advice, if you are planning a sex-toy party, get one of those big containers of Barbicide they use to disinfect the combs in the locker room at the health club. After each use, toss the sex toy in there and you're all set.

Oh, and one more tip about your next sex-toy party—have it catered. You don't want to have to worry about things in the kitchen. You should spend the time with your friends.

Doctor Approved

While some women are too cavalier in their use of sexual aids, others are a bit overly cautious. The woman sitting fully clothed in the exam room certainly was. The doctor had been puzzled when he checked her chart before entering the room. Dr. G. noticed that the patient wasn't due for an annual exam for five more months. She wasn't pregnant, so he was uncertain exactly why she was here. After an exchange of pleasantries, the doctor asked how he could help the woman. She reached into her purse and pulled out a large dildo.

"Is this O.K.?" she asked.

"O.K.? For, for what?" stammered the confused doctor.

"Just to use."

"I don't see why not."

"Is it safe?"

"I feel like I'm in *Marathon Man*."

"What?"

"Never mind. Go ahead and use it. It's safe. Is that it?"

"Yes. Thank you."

That was all she had made the appointment for. She needed to get her dildo approved. How long before some dildo manufacturer jumps on this and markets a whole line of doctor-recommended dildoes and vibrators? How about the advertising tag line—"Doctor-tested Acme vibrator. Women love it . . . Doctors trust it."

Diploma . . .tic

An excruciatingly long wait aside, you probably never paid much attention to the diplomas hanging on the wall of your OB's office. Maybe a quick glance to see where she went to med school or to see if you have any recollection of that semester of Latin. Disappointed that diplomas don't conjugate "agricolae" you move on, not once concerned whether or not one of those diplomas is from the Board of Gynecologists. That's the big one. Not in size but in importance, because that one is the actual license to practice medicine. Completing med school doesn't earn it. Finishing a residency program doesn't qualify you. You only get it when you pass a couple of dreaded tests.

Upon completing residency, new OB/GYNs take a comprehensive written exam. Think of it as a grueling S.A.T.-type of exam covering the myriad situations an OB might face. A sample question might be one of those relationship questions such as:

Baby:Mommy:
   A. Cub:Bear
   B. Baby:Bear
   C. Insurance:Mommy
   D. Fetus:Womb.

The correct answer, of course, is C. Insurance and the baby are two things you have to get out of the mommy. If they pass the written exam, then recent grads haven't wasted the past eight years of training. They are allowed then to go out into the world and practice medicine in their chosen field. They also must prepare for the next exam, an oral one, which comes up in two and a half years.

The long break before the oral exam is time in which doctors are supposed to build a case list of every patient they see for the first year and a half. This case list provides fodder for intense grilling by established and esteemed OB/GYNs who make you justify your actions. It would be hard enough if it were your peers questioning you, but when someone you have idolized as a scholar walks into that room with your future in his hands, you can't help but feel underprepared.

As in most professions, there is an elite in the medical world. Academicians can be out of touch with the day-to-day running of a medical practice. Still, there are those special few who wrote an important textbook or were responsible for a new drug or different procedure. Those few inspire the reverence of their colleagues and command fear as inquisitors at the oral board exam.

Karen was quizzed by someone she knew to be a famous doctor. He had invented or discovered something . . . the scalpel . . . birth control . . . began with a "C" . . . Oh yes, Dr. Cee. Invented the C-section. Happened by accident one night in his lab, or so the story goes. Well, Karen was flabbergasted. Couldn't answer a question. You'd have thought she was being interrogated by GOD HIMSELF!

"Dost thou dare to use forceps in the birth of the child in case number 107?" he thundered.

"The child would not come forth. Woe is me, for I am but flesh and blood and will return to dust." answered Karen.

"And who is the creator of all surgical instruments?" he roared.

"You are, my lord." was Karen's sheepish reply.

"Then you have passed this test, but you face one more before you can gain your license. Go forth, my child, and bring me the broomstick of the Wicked Witch of the West."

Well, that was no easy task, mind you, what with those fly-ing monkeys and all. But Karen did it, and now she's a full-fledged wizard . . . er, doctor, and she has the brain . . . um, diploma to prove it.

Nervous Wreck

A Harvard diploma would not have calmed this patient down. The whole idea of merely being at the gynecologist's was enough to get her shaking. Today, though, she was in full dread, anticipating a procedure called an endometrial biopsy. It's a common office procedure that is done when women have irregular periods. She was told that it may cause some cramping, but most women have only mild discomfort. She didn't believe it for a minute. Lying on the table, waiting for the doctor, she imagined the horrific pain that was certain to ensue.

The doctor came in and tried to calm the patient. He was moderately successful and began the biopsy. With the first twinge of a cramp, the woman hyperventilated. The second cramp caused her to pass out. Now, some people go limp when they pass out. Others begin to spasm. This patient was of the latter. She spasmed and her legs shot straight up. They wrapped around the doctor's neck and became stiff, putting him in an inescapable headlock. Unable to extricate himself, the doctor yelled for his brand-new assistant.

When the assistant came in she was taken aback by her new boss' compromised position.

"Doctor! What are you doing?!" she exclaimed, knowing that his stance was not sanctioned by the medical profession.

"Let's put it this way. If we were wrestling, I'd be losing." replied the entrapped doctor. He then tagged his assistant, who freed him from the hold, and they went on to complete the biopsy and win the match.

Crime and Punishment

Let's say you were a criminal. A burglar. Or a robber. A nice, reasonable clear-thinking criminal. What would you choose to rob? Homes, because of the lack of security? Banks, because that's where the money is? Perhaps art museums, for the glamour and the challenge. If you said any of the above, you would be welcomed by the respected American criminal community and any fraternal orders they happen to have. On the other hand, if you said "doctors' offices," your fellow thieves might not be ready to let you in on the secret handshake.

There wouldn't seem to be much worth pilfering from the doctor's office, and yet things disappear all the time. The stuff is expensive, no doubt, but of value to anyone other than a doctor? I doubt it. Other than serving its intended purpose, what someone would want a speculum for I wouldn't speculate. Folks, if you like to play doctor at home, remember, you don't need the tools. "It's fun to use your imagination." Oh my God, I've had too much to drink. I'm quoting Barney again.

The most common item that disappears is a doptone. That's the device that is used to hear the baby's heartbeat starting at close to three months. Hearing the heartbeat is a thrilling moment for most mothers. It's the first tangible confirmation that there is another human being growing inside and, to many parents-to-be, that rhythm is music that they want to play over and over. Without the doptone, however, it's like having a CD with no CD player. So some patients can't resist grabbing the doptone after the doctor leaves the exam room.

Then they get home and realize they now have a CD, a CD player, but no damn instructions on how to operate the CD player. What they forgot to steal was the conductive jelly that goes with the doptone.

Even if they had the jelly and were as proficient at finding the heartbeat as the doctor was, what would they have then? I'll tell you what they'd have. They'd have a CD player with a vast collection of ONE CD! That same heartbeat that was music to their ears gets redundant pretty quickly when it's the only thing to play. The mother-to-be would find out that even in utero, children can get quite annoying as they repeat the same thing over and over. Think of that heartbeat as the voice of a two-year-old rhythmically repeating, "Look Mommy . . . look mommy . . . look mommy . . . look mommy . . ." demanding that you watch him perform some amazing physical feat like spinning around in a circle while you're trying to finish your dissertation or do your taxes or just have five minutes to read the damn paper for once without having to watch the whirling dervish show with performances every half hour! That would stop those doptones from walking out of the office.

Lesser items are probably taken and not even noticed by the doctors. People take rubber gloves, needles and syringes and sample packs of birth control pills. I think it relates back to childhood, when the pediatrician gives you a treat because you had to get a shot. You got a piece of candy or a sticker to make you forget the pain. Some people can't accept that they have grown out of that. They are still looking for their surprise, and taking a rubber glove makes them feel better. That's my own little psychoanalysis of the cause of this kleptomania.

(Keep in mind, this analysis is coming from a man who falls for the old distraction game every time my kids get a shot. The nurse will have my daughter play with a balloon and surreptitiously stick her with a needle. I'm as intent on the balloon as my daughter and wonder why she started crying all of a sudden. I'm not very sophisticated. I suspect that on my next physical, the doctor could have me tossing a balloon and the next thing I'd say is, "Whoa, doc, that's my prostate you're holding. Why didn't you tell me?" "We find it goes easier this way," he would explain.)

Birth control pills are the only item whose theft makes some sense to me. They are a common need and are expensive. I don't know how much a diaphragm costs, but it must be expensive too. That would explain why one doctor found it necessary to put a penny-size hole in the middle of the one she uses as a demonstration model. Some previous models had been stolen, and the physician was hoping that the rather obvious hole would discourage others from swiping this model. It worked. Not without a side effect, however. One patient came back to the doctor a few months after being fitted for her diaphragm and was pregnant. The doctor wondered if the patient had had any difficulty with her diaphragm.

"No," said the patient. "I even cut out the little hole in the middle to make sure it looked just like yours."

Bad . . . Umm . . . Timing

In my mind, I'm always preparing for the most unlikely, horrible things to happen to me. Every time I visit California, I'm certain the next earthquake is going to hit. Every airplane I fly is sure to have the engine fall off. Every time I step on an elevator, I just know the cable will snap. Oddly, I never envision being harmed by any of these things. I always concoct some sort of escape plan whereby I save myself. For example, when the elevator cable snaps, I simply wait until the elevator is almost to the bottom and then I JUMP, so that I'm really only falling a few feet. I've been told that the laws of physics dictate otherwise, so I've decided that what I would really do if the elevator cable snaps is SCREAM and fall to my death. That's my plan.

The point of all this is that most of the time, the catastrophe doesn't happen. Most of us aren't in the wrong place at the wrong time. But there are no stories in that, are there? To get in this book, you have to be in the right place at the wrong time. Or is it the wrong place at the right time? Whatever, here are a few women caught in natural or manmade disasters where things went all wrong, all right?

Lucy had rearranged her life around her doctor's appointment. The appointment had been made months in advance, but no time was going to be a good time for the go-go lawyer. (She didn't represent go-go girls. A better choice would have been to call her an "on-the-go" lawyer.) In fact, if Lucy could get out of there in time she could get to a meeting that had come up just hours earlier. She was happy to see the doctor walk into the exam room right on schedule. After the standard few questions, Lucy got in the stirrups, and just as she did, the power blew and the room went dark. A little daylight seeped through the curtained window. Confusion swept through the office, and no one was certain when the power would return. So the doctor told Lucy to get dressed and call for another appointment.

Lucy would have none of that. She couldn't afford to forego another work afternoon. She insisted that the doctor examine her right then. The doctor tried to talk her out of it, but Lucy was adamant. She didn't care if the doctor opened the shade for some light, so he did. That wasn't enough, so he got a flashlight. So there she was, with her legs spread wide to the window and a flashlight shining on her privates. People in the parking lot who looked up probably thought they were in Amsterdam.

While it's bad timing to be in the stirrups when the lights go out, I submit that it's even worse when the fire alarm sounds. There is no great urgency in a power failure. When that horn blasts, however, it could mean you only have a few seconds to get out safely. Or it could mean that there's a fire drill. When you are up in the stirrups just about to be examined, it's tempting to assume that it's a false alarm. When this happened to Karen and a patient, they wavered for a second.

KAREN: It's probably just a drill.
PATIENT: Does the alarm go off often?
KAREN: It's never gone off before.
PATIENT: So you think we should go?
KAREN: Well, let's look at the consequences. If it's just a drill and you bother to get dressed, go outside, wait and then have to come back in and get back in the stirrups, then all you've had is a little inconvenience. On the other hand, if you don't go and it is a fire, you die.

Karen and the patient thought about it for a beat, looked at each other and in unison said, "Aww, let's finish the exam." All those years of training in elementary school had reinforced the idea that when that alarm goes off, it's just a drill. Fortunately for them, it was.

The fire department became part of the obstetrics team on another occasion that also didn't involve a real fire. Snow precipitated this incident. A surprise Thanksgiving Day storm had caught the road maintenance division unprepared. The workers were on holiday, and by the time anyone realized that the storm was going to bring 40 inches of snow instead of the forecast quarter inch, it was impossible for any of the plow drivers to even get to their plows. The city was at a standstill for days.

Dr. Dave had gone in to do a delivery late that Thanksgiving morning. Six hours later he was done with the delivery, but stuck at the hospital thanks to the snow. He would be there for three days. On day two, he got a page that one of his patients was in labor and en route to the hospital. He wasn't sure how she was going to get to the hospital through the snow. Then he looked out his fifth-floor window and could see a fire truck about a mile away. The fire truck was loaded with one driver, five men and five shovels. It moved along in fits and starts as the men would jump out, shovel, hop back on the truck, drive the couple of feet and repeat the process—all the while panicking to get this laboring patient to the hospital on time. It's an odd thing about firemen; they will jump into a blazing building to pull a baby out of a fire, but they'd rather shovel the city than pull a baby out of a delivering woman.

Doctor Dave watched the slow progress from his window. It took a couple of hours to get her there. He met the exhausted firemen in the lobby to inform them that the elevators weren't working. The firemen took turns carrying the woman up the five flights of stairs. Totally spent, the firemen collapsed in a waiting room, hoping to find their effort rewarded with a quickly delivered, healthy baby. In just five minutes, Doctor Dave returned with the news. She was in false labor. She could go home. If they wanted to take her.

Tattoos and Body Piercing

I know. This is the chapter that got you to buy this book. You want to know what tattoos women have and where. Pure prurient interest. Maybe you're a woman looking for ideas. Maybe you're a man who has some ideas and wants to know if he has any chance of meeting a woman who could fulfill those ideas. Maybe you are a woman who has a tattoo and you're wondering if there are any other women out there who've gotten as drunk as you. The answer is, yes there are. And while having a tattoo or jewelry planted on or near your privates may still be a defiant act in America, it is embedded in the cultures of many societies.

Anthropologists have discovered several tribal groups and religions where the social hierarchy is based on sexual prowess. Often this is determined by number of offspring, but for males it can be predicated on number of conquests. With each successive conquest, the males get another tattoo. Each successive tattoo is placed closer to the genitals. A chief is chosen from among the males who have tattoos on their penises. Not to editorialize, but it all sounds quite primitive. Unlike America. Here we have a democracy, where we discuss grand ideas of liberty and justice and rights and then VOTE for a chief with distinguishing marks on his penis. We have come a long way.

At least I understand men getting tattoos. Most of us have such a hard time expressing ourselves—who we are, what we're all about—that a picture or two can be helpful. A guy could wear a T-shirt with a picture of a naked woman on a motorcycle, but sometimes you have to change shirts. How do you make a statement then? How do people know what you're all about? Two identical shirts? No. You get the picture tattooed on your arm.

Women don't usually have that need. What they may often desire is the ability to stand out in a crowd. Tattoos and body piercing are another fashion accessory that can help catch the eye of a desired paramour. Of course, when it's positioned in an area that the man of your wishes won't see until you've gotten your wish, its value as a seduction device is nearly nil. In fact, it could serve as a sexual inhibitor rather than an aphrodisiac. That partially depends on what the tattoo is. If it's a skull and crossbones it might give a man pause. Even a cute little rose might distract a man from his passion. I know that if saw a tattoo I'd start thinking, "Wow, someone was down here a long time drawing that." That would lead to too many other questions and before you know it, the moment is lost.

Body piercing would be even worse. I would think it would induce immediate flaccidity in men. What man wouldn't initially think, "Boy! That's gotta hurt." Then the mind wanders to what it would feel like on us, and before you know it the guy is in therapy.

Some guys must like it, though. There must be men who would get really turned on by a tattoo on a woman's behind that said "This end up." But the woman who has one should realize she will be remembered forever as the "This end up" chick, and is that how you want to, ahem, end up?

Yet there are plenty of women who do get tattoos and piercings. I'm told that clitoral piercings can give added sexual stimulus. It only makes sense. I don't know about the sensations, but I'm sure a silver stud would help a man find the clitoris a lot faster. A little beacon to the man lost at sea.

So many women are getting piercings and tattoos that it has become a dilemma for gynecologists as to whether they should say something or not. There are two philosophies. My wife is very professional about it. She almost never says anything. She figures that as long as it doesn't affect the well-being of the patient, there is no need to delve into their personal lives.

A contrasting approach is taken by an OB/GYN in Florida. He figures that there is the danger of an insult if you don't say something. Fearing that the woman might feel slighted by a lack of interest, he always says something about their accouterments. If he can't muster a true compliment, he opens with, "That is some piece of work!" When he sees something spectacular he will call in the nurse to check it out. The women must not mind, because he says he is seeing more and more tattoos, from little roses to wild snakes and a naked lady riding a tongue. So many patients ask about piercing that if managed care reduces his income any further, he is going to open up a side business. The only thing that gives him pause is that nine out of ten women he asks about a tattoo or piercing have said they regret it. Given some of the tattoos gynecologists have seen, that's not surprising.

Among the more unique tattoos that I suspect will one day be regretted is one that said "JUST DO ME." It came complete with the Nike swoosh. I think it would have been even better if it had preceded that with a line, "QUIT READING ALREADY . . . ."

You don't want to get too wordy in a tattoo, though. One that was straight to the point and laid down the ground rules at the same time was the little man drawn high up on the woman's thigh. He was holding a red and white candy-striped ruler that reached above his head. Above the ruler read "MUST BE THIS TALL TO RIDE." Certainly one of the more popular attractions at Six Flags.

Another woman put her warning above her pubic hair. It said "PAY TOLL BELOW." I wonder if she offered a monthly pass so you wouldn't have to come up with exact change on every use.

The same location was used by a woman intent on defusing any liability concerns she had. Her cautionary inscription read "SLIPPERY WHEN WET."

Others are more artistic. One woman had a pretty little hummingbird right above the pubic hair. The bird was dipping its pointy beak to get nectar from her vagina. Some ornithologists go a lifetime without spotting this rare breed of vaginal-sucking hummingbird.

A religious, or perhaps irreligious woman had a likeness of Jesus tattooed just above her pubis. His beard was real.

A tattoo is usually not a sign of people who look far into the future. People with an inkling that they may go through changes in life are unlikely to get tattoos. People in their 80's are the ones who can feel comfortable in their self-awareness. They are the ones who should be getting tattoos, not teenagers. Teenagers about to get a tattoo don't consider how it will look if they ever have surgery or get pregnant. Otherwise, how do you explain the girl who got an elaborate tattoo of a dolphin on her lower belly? It was jumping out of the imaginary waters that lie just below her bikini line. A little more conservative than the previous examples, but also a little more problematic. She got pregnant. As her belly expanded so did the dolphin. It became more of a whale than a dolphin. When she needed a C-section, all the doctor could do was cut open the whale. I assume they named the child Jonah.

Anytime a tattoo needs to be cut into, there is the chance that it won't match up exactly right when it's put back together. If positioned properly, however, a tattoo can be a guide to better surgery. Just ask the woman who had to have surgery but was very adamant about where the doctor could cut. She gave herself a temporary tattoo in the form of a well-defined tan line. The doctor was not to cut above the tan line for risk that it would affect her livelihood. She was a stripper and positioned her tan to match her G-string.

A few other elaborate designs that gynecologists have run across include the woman whose inside thighs had eagle wings so that when she was spread-eagle, she truly was spread eagle. And an intriguing one was the woman with a Chinese symbol on her inner thigh, which the doctor could only guess meant dignity.

Then there are the women ready to profess their undying love to the man of the hour. That can be problematic, as the hour does change. One doctor had fun with a woman who came to him with a tattoo on her arm that said "Michael." He asked who Michael was, and she was a bit embarrassed, but said, "Oh, he's my first man." Upon further examination, along her bikini line was a tattoo that spelled out the name "Jones." "Oh," she said, that's my new man." The doctor laughed, thinking that she got a new tattoo for each man. He sat down on his stool and inserted the speculum. As he looked he asked, "Now then, who is Fred?"

Finally, my favorite is the woman who had tattooed her breasts with corresponding "RIGHT" and "LEFT" inscriptions. I can only presume it was to help her know which way to put them on in the morning.

Lunchtime is Drugtime

If you are in any OB's office around lunch time, there is a good chance you will be in the same room as a drug dealer. If you confront them over their evil ways, they will defend themselves by saying that they are just doing their job, and that there is a demand for their service, otherwise they wouldn't exist. Don't be fooled. They are pushers who are looking to get you hooked. Officially they are known as drug reps.

One day, they bring in a pizza for all the doctors. Just a little "thank you" for prescribing their companies' drugs. And the doctors think, "What harm could there be in eating a pizza?" So they eat it and what happens, a salad shows up next time with the pizza. And then, the pizza becomes lasagna which becomes a nice deli tray for everybody in the office, and before you know it, your doctor is hooked on the drug reps' lunches and he'll prescribe anything just to keep those meals coming. Then, if your doctor is a heavy prescriber, he'll get extra perks like dinners and tickets to ballgames or the theater.

As a doctor's spouse, I am all for this. Although I'm not around to appreciate the lunches, I welcome the tickets to concerts and sporting events and the nice dinners at restaurants that I would normally go to only on anniversaries that end in a zero. To comply with certain federal laws, the drug companies can't simply take the doctors out to dinner. They must make the dinners "educational." What that usually means is a five-minute talk by some doctor whose study proved that the company's birth control pill actually controlled birth nine out of ten times. That's worth sitting through for dinner at La Belle Eau.

On occasion we have to work harder for our meal than a brief lecture. Some speakers truly care about the product more than the free trip to the sunny Midwest in January. They will drone on and on about their miracle drug. I start questioning whether it's worth the dinner when the lecture drags on past 15 minutes. When the lecture goes over 20 minutes, I generally start to wish for the speaker to contract the disease his drug purports to cure. Depending on the subject matter, once the lecture is over, I sometimes don't want to eat, no matter how exclusive the restaurant. Karen and I were once at a dinner where the last ten minutes of the cumbersome lecture included slides of "rectal sigmoids." I can't tell you what they are, but let me give you my tip for a successful speaking engagement: Never end a talk with, "Enough about rectal sigmoids. Let's eat!"

Dinners and sporting events are nice, but I am just as happy for all the practical home products. The competition between the drug companies provides a continuous stream of T-shirts and carrying bags, sticky pads and phone cards. If the day should come when a drug company wants to give us a car emblazoned with advertisements for Terazol, well, I would not be beyond accepting it. Car racing does it, why shouldn't I?

I don't know what Terazol is, of course. I assume it's a birth control pill or vaginal cream. I wouldn't want to advertise Terazol if it's some brand name for a particularly dangerous drug. No matter how cool the make, driving the "Heroin" car, for example, would not be my style. Not to mention the hassles I'd get if I ever got pulled over for doing 20 MPH on the highway.

Advertising the wrong drug can be dangerous to my business as well. I often send out manuscripts to publishers or producers with a little handwritten note attached saying something clever like, "Here's my manuscript!" The note will be written on a sticky pad that trumpets birth control pills and vaginal cream on alternating pieces of paper. I take the risk that my urgent message might be overlooked by a woman recipient with an infection who is reminded by my sticky pad of her itching. Or, imagine the emotional turmoil a birth control pill sticky note might give to the woman who just found out she is carrying an unwanted pregnancy. My manuscript would not get a fair read. You can see how discriminating I have to be.

Social situations can have their minefields also. Once, I was proudly displaying to a woman friend my free 10-minute phone card with the name of a popular pill on it. Her face soured with disgust as she told me that she didn't like that phone card because it gave her cramps.

Condomania

Without going into unnecessary detail, you must realize that there are often times when a probe is used in an office exam. In the name of cleanliness and sterilization, a condom will be used to cover the probe. In this manner a gynecologist's office can go through a fair number of condoms in a month. If they aren't careful about their inventory, they can unexpectedly run out. That's what happened one day at Karen's office. Fortunately, a drugstore is around the corner. It's hard for any of the doctors to get away in the middle of the day, so one of Karen's partners sent the office manager to buy some condoms.

The eight-months-pregnant office manager.

For a couple gross of condoms.

I'm a grown man who has done it plenty of times, but I'm still a bit embarrassed when I buy condoms. Maybe that's because I'd never bought them in gross lots before. Maybe that would make me proud. I'd walk in with my chest puffed out and announce loudly to the clerk and anyone nearby, "Yes, I'd like a couple gross of condoms, and then I'll be back next week for more. I'm a busy man."

This woman didn't do that. She waddled in, big belly and all, and politely asked the pharmacist for the condoms. The pharmacist couldn't help himself and commented, "I think it's a little late for these, ma'am."

You Put What? Where?

There has been a series of popular books about home remedies for common ailments. The authors give medical advice wherein common household items are used for purposes other than what the instructions might say. For example, cayenne pepper is supposed to stop the pain of a cut, washing cloth diapers in vinegar prevents diaper rash, and drinking a half dozen shots of tequila with a beer chaser will make all your troubles disappear, at least until the morning.

Baking soda seems to be the most nimble of products. It has myriad uses. It calms poison ivy, absorbs odors, polishes teeth and, I didn't realize this, but you can actually bake with baking soda. You could bake a batch of cookies and then use them as little air fresheners throughout the house.

The fact that these items are in a book suggests that, either it's all one big practical joke to get the public to do silly stuff, or someone has actually tried these things out. Someone, unprovoked, put mayonnaise in their hair for conditioner. I don't know if it was inspiration, or they had soap in their eyes, or they were lacking for cupboard space, but someone first tried this. When it works, it seems like nothing less than an inspiration. What we don't see is all the people trying to get Wishbone Italian out of their hair while they say to themselves, "What was I thinking?" The success of these books only leads to more attempts to do the foolish. It's the gynecologist who often gets to see the results.

One of the most common household remedies resulting in a trip to the doctor's is yogurt. Folklore has it that yogurt will effectively battle a yeast infection. In fact, yogurt can be effective medicine as long as the discomfort is truly caused by a yeast infection. The home remedy fails when the same symptoms are a result of bacteria. When applied to a bacterial infection, yogurt can exacerbate the problem. Unless you can diagnose your ailment with certainty, it's best to consult your doctor and get a prescription yogurt. Most often these will be plain or vanilla and not the "fruit on the bottom" kind.

I assume the main reason women resort to something in their fridge instead of calling the doctor is that they need immediate relief from the symptoms. When a bad bout of itching strikes, relief is paramount, and proximity prevails over prudence. If nothing in the fridge seems like it could stop the itching, well the next logical place to look would be—cleaning supplies. One woman decided that Lysol would do the trick. Why not? It disinfects. Another woman felt that Mop & Glo was the ideal product to douche with. I guess it stopped the itching, gave her a nice shine and protected against those annoying scuff marks. It also was the cause of an office visit to take care of an unusual discharge.

When not trying to alleviate an ailment, there are women who turn to household items for emergency lubrication. Having sex on the kitchen table apparently is not just a fantasy, it's also a convenience. Think of all the lubricants that are readily accessible without having to roll off the counter. One woman found happiness with corn oil. In fact she used a low-fat corn oil blend. As she explained to her gynecologist, she felt it important to reduce the polyunsaturated fats she was putting in her vagina.

If you use something from the kitchen shelf to aid in sexual activity, then you are probably willing to use something from another shelf for birth control. The woman showed up at the hospital complaining of an unusual discharge. The doctor asked her a few questions before examining her, as to the extent, onset and color of the discharge. Her response to color was purple. The doctor stopped. "Are you using birth control?" "Yes," the woman replied proudly. I was just fitted for a diaphragm." The nurse told me to use whatever jelly I had around the house. All I had was grape."

Doctors need to be pretty good sleuths when women show up with various problems resulting from the use of some household items. Yogurts, oils and Lysol are all at least semi-liquid and will dissipate in the body quickly. If the patient doesn't tell the doctor that they used some odd product—and obviously they didn't think it was a concern when they used it—the doctor may not be able to figure it out. Solids are another matter. When, like one doctor, you find a whiffle ball in someone's vagina, you don't need to know why it's there. You just need to know it can't stay there. Vibrators seem to get stuck so often they should probably come with some kind of emergency release strap. And while the woman noted above may not have been wise about using grape jelly, at least she saw a doctor to get fitted for a diaphragm. One woman, obviously on the spur of the moment, found a green toy octopus with suction cups for tentacles, and felt that would do the job and stay in with all the jostling it might receive. It stayed in so well, she had to go to the hospital to have a disbelieving ER nurse remove it. It's not true that the James Bond movie *Octopussy* was based on her case.

Then there was the woman whose troubles turned out to be caused by a wad of money that she had stashed in the best hiding place she could find. I imagine the doctor was thrilled that he not only cured his patient, but got paid in cash.

At least the money, whiffle ball and octopus were immediately identifiable. One doctor found a large mass in a 50-year-old patient who had not complained of any pain. He was attempting to get a small piece of the mass for a biopsy to see if it was cancerous, when he found the whole mass was loose.

He removed it and sent it to the pathology lab right away. While it was being diagnosed, the gynecologist gently began discussing with the patient the possibility of cancer and let her know that he was calling an oncologist for a consult. The woman was distraught and needed to know how this could have happened. She offered one possibility.

"Do you think it could have been caused by the bacon, doctor?

"Well, it's been suggested that a diet heavy in meat may have some correlation, but . . . "

"No. Not eating bacon. The bacon I put in my vagina."

"The WHAT?"

"I put bacon in my vagina to keep myself moist. My momma taught it to me. I've been doing it ever since. I keep it fresh. I change the bacon once a month."

The doctor excused himself and ran back to the lab to take another look at the mass. He pulled on it and it started to unravel. It kept unrolling until he was able to lay it flat. If it ever belonged to Bob Evans, he sure wouldn't claim it now, but it was unquestionably a piece of bacon. The biopsy results came back, and both doctor and patient were relieved to hear that the bacon was not malignant. However, they were sure the pig's condition was terminal.

Finally, I must tell the story of the woman who showed up at her doctor's complaining of vines growing from her vagina. Uncertain of what she meant, her doctor proceeded to do a pelvic exam and found that her problem was in fact what is medically known as "vines growing out of the vagina." The patient was at an advanced age and sought to remedy the underlying condition that her uterus was falling out. She had found that a sweet potato served as a passable pessary. The dark, moist conditions had caused the sweet potato to branch out into her pants. Bacon and sweet potatoes. My friends, when it comes to gynecological oddities, that is the meat and potatoes.

The Password Is . . .

Many of the words that need to be used at the gynecologist's office are hard to say. They aren't difficult to pronounce, they just carry a burden of emotional baggage. These are words we giggle at as kids and blush at as adults. For example, a seemingly simple word like: vagina. Hard to say. Easy to write. Hard to feel comfortable putting it in a conversation. There's really only one person who can comfortably say the vocabulary used at the gynecologists—Mister Rogers. He should do a little video for the waiting room, "Today, neighbors, we're going to take a trip to the gynecologist's office. Can you say 'Va-gina'? That's good, neighbor."

Until then, embarrassed women will continue to use euphemisms to describe their private parts. It seems more ladylike. "Down there" is a common reference. Fortunately for the patients who use that expression, the doctors seem to know how far down there they have to look. That avoids the "you're getting warmer, warmer, now colder, colder" game that would prove even more embarrassing than the actual exam. "Down under" is another nickname. If you are worried about things that are happening down under, then you should just avoid Australia altogether.

Most common after the directional moniker is the third-person designation. This could be "my friend," "my sister" or one woman simply uses the pronoun "she." When you say, "She's been having a problem" don't be surprised if your doctor pauses to look around the room for a second to see if someone else is there.

The more unusual names take a little longer to figure out. Usually, the word in a sentence that doesn't make sense is the body part. See if you can find the substitute for vagina in this complaint to the doctor—"I've got stuff coming from my kooch." If you said "kooch," congratulations, you are well on your way to a career in medicine. Now here's one for you second-year students—"You can play with my playpen, but don't touch my playground." Got a little tougher, didn't it? That was said by a woman who was told that she needed a hysterectomy. Playpen is uterus, playground means vagina. Makes perfect sense now, doesn't it? Other common terms for vagina include: "Possibility," "Thing" and "Stuff." Let's hope you don't get any stuff in your stuff, but we all know it's a possibility.

An even greater challenge for the doctor than understanding these terms is relating back to the patient in language that they can understand. Doctors have become comfortable with standard names for body parts. When someone tells them their "kitty cat's gone and catch a cold" they know that means she's having a vaginal discharge, but it's still hard to explain to the woman that her "kitty cat's gonna have to go to sleep for a while to get over that cold."

Worse than body parts is when a physician is approached for a second opinion and has to decipher the patient's vernacular for medical procedures and complications. Epidurals become "epidermals," fibroids on the uterus become "fireballs on the Eucharist" and blood clots have turned into "blood clogs." Who wants to wear a pair of those? One patient, upon being corrected and told that it's clots and not clogs, told the doctor, "Look, I don't know the technical terms . . . ."

Some other misconstrued words that have been deciphered with the discovery of the Rosetta Stone include:

Contraptions = contractions
Gongaria = Gonorrhea
Tubalization = Tubal Ligation

Very close veins = Varicose veins
Smiling Mighty Jesus = Spinal Meningitis
Sick as Hell Anemia = Sickle Cell Anemia
That Mexican Disease = Trichomonas

For patients who don't have the words, talking to the doctor must be as frustrating as a trip to France—they don't seem to understand, even when you talk louder. One doctor got one of those middle-of-the-night phone calls from a woman asking if she could get pregnant if she had "sex from behind." The doctor is trying to figure out if she had sex doggy style or if she had anal intercourse. She clearly didn't know the words "vagina" or "anal." Finally, her annoyed boyfriend took the phone to tell the doctor that he had "put his thing in her butt, COULD SHE GET PREGNANT?!" Explained in those terms, the doctor understood it loud and clear.

A little handbook of useful phrases in patientese would be a bestseller for doctors. That way, when a patient tells them they have "rats in their pajamas" they could look it up instead of spending time trying to tell the patient that they should wash their pajamas.

"No, doctor. I have rats in my pajamas!" insisted the patient.

"Well, why do you say that?" asked the befuddled doc.

"Because every time my husband is in my pajamas he gets bit."

"You're saying you have pain with intercourse?"

"I'm saying, I have rats in my pajamas."

Seeing that this was going nowhere, the doctor decided to do a digital exam. He stuck his finger in and "Ouch!" he got bit. Turned out that a needle had broken off during her recent episiotomy and was lodged so that it would prick her husband's prick during intercourse. Since there was no previous official term for it, a needle in the vagina is now officially known in the lingo as "rats in the pajamas."

Generally, doctors learn the language of their patient base in due time, and confusion is avoided. Over time the language of the medical and the patient worlds should converge as patients get better educated and doctors become more accepting. Until then we can revel in our regional and cultural language barriers that produced the following classic exchange: A transplanted Yankee was trying to determine the extent of his native Southern patient's bleeding.

"How's your flow?" he asked.

The woman thought for a second, trying to make the connection, but couldn't.

"My flo? My flo is linoleum . . . why do you ask?

Movies of the Week

The things women reveal to their doctors are incredible. Apparently nothing is so personal or private that it can't be told to the gynecologist. It doesn't matter that the information has no medical significance. It seems a lot of women want to unburden themselves to their OB/GYN. As much as you may feel your OB is your friend and confidant, you don't need to tell him everything. Your OB needs only so much information. Your medical history may be interrelated with your sexual history, but the doctor doesn't need to know exactly who you've been sleeping with or the details of the night you got pregnant. The doctor's day would move a lot faster if some patients didn't confuse their OB with their therapist. Indeed, there are physician instruction manuals on how to quickly get out of the exam room without seeming insensitive. Invariably, however, there is at least one patient a day who won't let the doctor out of the room.

The doctor knows he's going to hear some convoluted triangle story when a newly pregnant patient wants to know exactly when they got pregnant. Exactly. To the day. Or even hour. Patients with stable, monogamous relationships don't seek this information. Patients who are with John on Tuesdays and Bill on Thursdays find it of utter importance. Sadly, the doctor can only give a ballpark estimate. Then it's wait until the blood test. Of course, you'd have to have the father's blood tested too, and that might arouse some suspicion in the fellows. So, if you are in that situation, and you care who the father is, I suggest you let the men know about each other right away. They have the same taste in women, so who knows, maybe they will become friends. And soon the lion will lie down with the lamb, and men will beat their swords into ploughshares. Hey look, a flying pig!

One week Karen had vacation and sat down in the afternoon to catch up on some soap operas. She turned them off when she found the stories weren't half as intriguing as the relationships her patients told her about. Soap operas are drawn-out melodramas of daily relationships. Karen's stories were more appropriate for the sensational one-time performances—her stories were movies of the week.

So, just when you thought all those movies of the week were getting a little ridiculous, along comes this chapter. You know the movies I'm talking about, or at least the promos for the movies I'm talking about. The quick-cut scenes of tears and hugging as the *basso profundo* voice-over bellows, "Forced to choose between the daughter she loved and the passion she could never control. A woman's struggle with a secret in her heart, the child she never knew and one last candy bar. Obsession with Chocolate, This Friday, 8 Eastern on ABC. A true story."

If your story isn't compelling enough to put you on the Jerry Springer Show, you can always hope for a Movie of the Week. So, I now present promos for some amazing, but honestly true stories of people with illicit affairs and convoluted relationships, revealed by women at the doctor's office for no other reason than the door was closed and her pants were off.

APPEARING SOON:
- Carla's baby boy was the spitting image of her husband, Tom. She hoped that he wouldn't notice that the little boy was also the spitting image of Tom's father. This Tuesday night, a television affair for the whole family, *Either Way It's a Smith.*
- She divorced her husband for another man. But that did-

n't mean she couldn't go back to him on a lonely night when she was fertile. Will the current husband realize the baby is carrying *'Ex' Chromosomes?* Wednesday, 7 Pacific.

- After years of infertility, her husband felt he didn't need protection, even when he had an affair. That's when he found out his sperm was good. Now *she* claims custody of the other woman's baby. Watch, *It Ain't Me Babe.* Thursday on NBC.

- Three girls are tough enough to handle, but the Watsons always wanted a boy, so they thought they would try one more time. They get their precious boy, but only at a horrible price. Watch a family of five turn into the family from hell when Mom has spontaneous triplets, in the CBS movie *Eight is a Zoo.*

- She was a loving woman. She loved her husband. She loved her father. And she showed her love in the same way. Now, will she have enough love for her baby son, even though she doesn't know which one's the dad? Probably when he's old enough. Watch *Ball in the Family*, Wed. at 11 on FOX. Parental indiscretion advised.

- When Bob had a vasectomy, he was told there was a small chance it could fail. What are the chances Julie, his now-pregnant wife, can convince him that the baby is his? Much better if her doctor could explain it to the husband.
  (CLIP FROM FILM)
  WOMAN (crying): "Doctor, what are you going to tell my husband?"
  DOCTOR: "Me? I'm not telling him anything."
  The world premiere of *Reversal of Vasectomy of Fortune* on WB. Check local listings.

- When the labor pains started, Lisa knew the moment of truth had arrived. Two men loved her. Would either one still love her after tonight? It all depended on what color the baby came out. Join us this Saturday at 6 for a very special edition of *The Match Game*. Special appearance by Gene Rayburn as the obstetrician.

- John and Marsha wanted a baby, but John's guys weren't good swimmers. They picked a daddy from a list. Marsha picked up a lover in a bar. Now, which stranger is the father? All Marsha can do is look at her list, check it twice and try to figure out if it's naughty or nice. If it's the wrong one, John will leave. Watch *People are Estranged When it's a Stranger*. Music by the Doors. CBS Sunday.

Table for Two

There are all kinds of sophisticated pieces of machinery in an OB/GYN's office. You would think that the exam table would be one of the simpler ones, but it's not necessarily so. Your doctor's office may have one of those Craftmatic-designed tables that adjusts up and down. If you're really lucky, your doctor will have put it on a Clapper, so you can entertain yourself while you wait. The tables that do have a hydraulic system are used for certain office procedures, one of the most common of which is a colposcopy. If you haven't had a colposcopy, don't feel left out. You don't want one. In fact, I would say as a rule you don't want anything ending in "oscopy" except maybe an extra DOS copy in case your computer crashes. But that's it, and believe me, that one was a reach.

A colposcopy is done when a woman has an abnormal Pap smear and needs her cervix examined more closely to see if there might be something wrong. What could be a closer exam than the normal pelvic exam the gynecologist gives? How about if he does the exam looking through an instrument that enlarges your genitals to 15 times their normal size? Pretty scary. Kind of like watching a porno flick in an IMAX theater.

The colposcope itself looks like one of those ubiquitous swiveling metal viewing binoculars that stand at the ledge of the Grand Canyon and every other national monument. For our story, Audrey will play the part of the woman, while her genitals will play the part of the Grand Canyon. Young Doctor

Mike will play the part of the tourist with a handful of quarters.

So there he was, at the end of the table, between the woman's legs, sitting on one of those stools that scoots around on wheels and is used on slow days for stool races around the office. He's looking through his 3-D Viewmaster. Audrey was a considerable 250 pounds or so. I'm not sure of her exact weight but it was at least one more pound than that table could handle.

There was a sudden noise, and before he could move, the front end of the table collapsed. The table is on two hydraulics, kind of like a car lift in a mechanic's garage, and the front end had broken. Because only one end collapsed, it meant that Audrey's legs and bottom were now at a downward angle. When it collapsed it also landed on Doctor Mike's feet, causing some pain and trapping him in his position at the end of the table. The deli paper which is placed underneath a patient on the table does not provide enough friction to keep someone from sliding, ever so slowly, down the vinyl-topped table.

It had to have been like being stuck in quicksand. Slowly, the woman began sliding down on top of her trapped doctor. He would try to struggle to get away, but each movement of his caused her to sink further toward him. Meanwhile, having never had a colposcopy before, Audrey is wondering if this is part of the procedure.

The Grand Canyon growing ever larger by the second, Doctor Mike cried for help, knowing that soon he would be in over his neck, unable to breathe. Fortunately, his office staff heard his cries and rushed in to save him—as soon as they extracted a promise that he would give them all a raise.

Miss-Conception

I think it's common knowledge that not everyone possesses common knowledge. Physicians, on the whole, seem unaware of this—ipso facto, you could say that doctors don't have common knowledge. What they do have is uncommon knowledge which they mistakenly think is common. That's why they don't always properly explain things, or are always telling us things they think we understand, when, in reality, we have no idea what they're talking about. Fortunately, the average patient's common knowledge gets them through. What is scary is when the doctor fails to sufficiently communicate his uncommon knowledge to the patient who has an uncommon lack of knowledge. More often than not, the subject area where this knowledge discrepancy occurs is birth control.

One lady showed up at the doctor's office pregnant, wondering what could have gone wrong, for she had been taking the pill every day. A few inquiries by the doctor revealed that although she had been taking the pill daily, she had been taking it vaginally. And probably not even with a glass of water. Another pregnant woman couldn't understand her predicament, as she had been taking the pill "every time my boyfriend and I have sex."

The pill isn't the only birth control method to befuddle. As is the nature of the practice, one patient was confiding with her OB about an extramarital affair. (A confusing term in itself. I was always told "extra" was good. I was encouraged to take extra-curricular activities during my school years, to go the extra mile and now I'm told extra isn't good when it comes to marital? Who can blame people for fooling around?) The OB was non-judgmental, but cautioned the patient that she should be using birth control. The patient dismissed the doctor's concerns. "I don't worry about that," she said. "My husband had a vasectomy."

Conception seems to be the major area of confusion. I myself am confused. What puzzles me is how so many kids could skip sex-ed class. That would be the only explanation for a question one woman posed. She wondered if having sex while she was pregnant could possibly plant another baby right behind the one already in there. That's a good premise for a sci-fi horror flick—sequential births. "The babies that just kept coming." Aggghhh!

Last Patient of the Day

A doctor was running behind schedule at the office and had to rush to the hospital as soon as he was done. His last office patient sat before him complaining of a discharge. She added that she also had a bad headache.

As I've said before, doctors don't like it when you add problems. This doctor was rather uncouth about it. He made the patient aware of his time pressure and told her she had to choose one—either the discharge or the headache.

She said, "I think they're related."

"And how is that?" the doctor hesitated to inquire.

"Well, I started having this thick, green discharge and a friend of mine said it was from a sexually transmitted disease, and when I told my boyfriend, he said 'Who you been sleeping with? What the hell did you give me?' And then he hit me over the head with a frying pan."

A Baby's First Slapstick

Timing Is Everything

There are web sites devoted to the beauty of having a home birth. It is filled with stories of mothers who had every intention of going to the hospital, didn't quite make it, but had a wonderful experience right in their own bed. You can click on a flowery fantasy about a woman giving birth by firelight as she gets a massage from her husband in a cozy, snowed-in, remote cabin. There are never any doctors in these visions, and the delivery is always complication-free and painless. Yeah, right.

As the ninth month approaches, women deserve to mentally frolic. While I can accept the simple pipe dream that the delivery will be an easy one, it takes too much imagination on my part to think that anyone would want to purposely go to a remote cabin for their delivery. That's not a fantasy of motherhood. That's the fantasy of surrogate motherhood. You and your husband go on a ski vacation while some other woman delivers your baby. That's an illusion I understand.

Today most babies are delivered in a hospital. I can see the appeal of a home birth, but those who have to do it at home probably dreamed of making it to the hospital before they had to push. I suspect that more women fantasize about getting to the hospital in time than fantasize about avoiding it altogether. While babies are born in cars in the hospital parking lot, it usually happens to fifth-time mothers whose labor is reduced to five minutes and who are so consumed by the other four kids that they don't even notice the contractions. First-time moms are the ones with the elaborate fantasies. They haven't been through it. They have no idea what they are getting into. Here's a first time mother-to-be's ideal delivery scenario:

"I'll be taking a leisurely walk near my neighborhood hospital one sunny afternoon, when I notice a couple of minor contractions. I note that they are only three minutes apart. I stride over to the hospital to find my doctor there. He advises me to call my husband to bring the bag that we had packed that morning. My husband arrives at the hospital within the half hour, just as the doctor checks me and finds that I am completely dilated and ready to push. Two quick pushes and a beautiful, healthy baby arrives."

Now, if you have ever delivered a baby or witnessed a delivery, you immediately picked up on the unlikelihood that the delivery will happen as this patient hopes. While parts of this dream delivery are plausible, the chances of them all occurring are infinitesimal when you consider the following probability charts:

OCCURRENCE	CHANCE OF OCCURRENCE
Labor begins in daylight	1 in 2
Reaches husband when labor begins	1 in 3
Fully dilated upon arrival at the hospital	1 in 50
Has bag ready for hospital stay	1 in 75
Packed bag that morning	1 in 500
In walking proximity of hospital when labor begins	1 in 1,257
Baby comes out in one push	1 in 50,000
Doctor present throughout labor	0 in HELL

Oddly enough, the most unlikely aspect of this delivery is the one most new patients expect to happen. They are under the impression that their doctor will be there for the duration of labor. It ain't gonna happen. Oh, I know—you have a great relationship with your doctor, and he's promised to see you through this life-giving experience. Trust me, when the big day arrives, he's got better things to do.

Your doctor's dream of the perfect delivery is in exact opposition to yours. His fantasy is to walk in on the last push, catch the baby and call it a night. To do this takes years of study, practice and a keen sense of timing. Even with all that, there is hardly a doctor who can't tell of a time the baby arrived before they did. Nevertheless, doctors will try to spend only as much time as is necessary with a patient. If a laboring patient arrives during the day, with the doctor already scheduled to be in the hospital anyway, attention will be considerable. The only distractions the doctor will have are: other patients, paperwork, phone calls and computer video games in the call room. If, however, you go into labor when your doctor is at home taking call, the distractions are immensely greater.

I'm guessing that Karen's standard procedure is similar to many other doctors'. When a patient in labor calls, Karen asks the patient for pertinent information. She asks about contraction intervals, prior deliveries, dilation at last check-up, proximity to the hospital, and general anxiety level of the patient. Karen then makes a judgment based on those factors and decides whether or not the patient should go to the hospital. If the woman is sent to the hospital, Karen will call the hospital and ask them to check her dilation. The only time she doesn't wait to hear from the hospital is if it's the woman's seventh child or beyond. If that's the case, she will rush to beat the woman to the hospital. That way, when the mother-to-be arrives, Karen can hold a net underneath her as she walks down the hospital corridor in case the baby falls out.

(This scenario is contingent on the patient calling to let Karen know that she is in labor. Sometimes that doesn't happen. Some patients just go into the hospital without ever calling their doctor to let them know. Don't do this. Obstetricians are highly trained, intelligent people. They are not psychic. If they were, you'd be in the hospital on your due date.)

When the hospital calls, they tell Karen how dilated the

woman is. If the woman is seven centimeters or greater, Karen will usually go in. Anything less and Karen must make another judgment as to how much time she has. The average first-time mom progresses at a rate of 1 centimeter per hour. Karen takes this into consideration, along with the following personal factors: Has she eaten dinner? Is the dinner I've prepared any better than what she could get at the hospital cafeteria? Are the kids behaving? Would leaving now prevent her from killing them? What's the wind-chill factor for the walk to the car? And if it's late at night, am I snoring so loudly that she would sleep better at the hospital?

Now, here's the medical secret that you won't get from any other source: The main objective for a doctor on call is to sleep as much as possible. The loudness of a spouse's snoring is the overriding factor in how quickly any doctor goes into the hospital. Most people with a tendency to snore will snore more after a big meal with some alcohol. Therefore, if you want to be sure your doctor will come in quickly, you should take your doctor and his/her spouse out on the town the same evening you plan on going into labor. Since you can't be sure when this will be, I suggest you do this every night, beginning two weeks before your due date. Since your pregnancy will probably have you feeling tired, and without much room for a lot of food, don't feel the need to join your doctor at these meals. Making the reservation and paying the bill will be sufficient. Then you can rest easy, and so can I.

Here's The Plan

Birth is a chaotic event. Yet there is a segment of generally well-educated women who walk into their doctor's office on their first pregnancy visit armed with a thing called "The Birth Plan." This plan informs the doctor of their wishes regarding the handling of the baby's birth. It will likely mention a preference for natural childbirth, offer specifics about how they want to cut the cord, maybe even request that the baby be delivered on a Wednesday. These are women who haven't yet grasped the idea that for the next 25 years, that child in their belly will be doing things to disrupt every plan they make. Birth is just the child's first act of mischief.

The most common request in these plans, is the desire for an epidural-free birth. Now, there are many women who are able to go through childbirth without drugs. Perhaps they have a high pain threshold. Maybe they have a body structure that makes delivery less painful. I don't know. But why decide that you can handle the pain before you've experienced its degree? No macho man ever went into the dentist's office to get a tooth removed and said, "No Novocaine for me, thank you. I want to get the full experience of the extraction."

Whatever the motivation for the drug-free delivery, some women are so intent on it that they have made pacts with their husbands. The woman will turn over complete control to her husband. She will tell the doctor that no matter how much pain she is in during labor, no matter how much she cries for an epidural, her husband is to see to it that she doesn't get one. This is also a well-known setup for a comedy routine.

Naturally (pun intended), during labor the pain begins to increase to the point where the woman asks for an epidural. The husband says "No." The wife says, "I know we had a plan . . . I'm changing the plan." The husband won't let her. The wife protests more vehemently as the pain grows. "I know I said that no matter how much I begged, don't give it to me. I'm not begging. I'M DEMANDING! GIVE ME THE #%@* EPIDURAL." The husband says, "You're doing fine, honey." And people wonder why the divorce rate is so high.

Couples should realize that when it comes to birth, it is folly to make plans for month nine in month one. It's great for patients to educate themselves as much as possible, but there is a fine line between discussing medical options with your doctor and dictating what you want. By all means, make your doctor aware of your wishes, ask a lot of questions, but listen to your doctor's opinions. She may have experience which is more valuable than what you've read in a book for mass consumption. A book like this one.

From the patient's perspective, it probably seems that many doctors won't give the patients any say in determining their own care. OBs certainly ought to listen to their patients and not dismiss their desires out of hand. If your doctor isn't attentive, you might remind him that millions of babies throughout the world are born without the aid of a doctor, so his services are most likely redundant. That will get you some fine care.

There are birth movements that truly prefer the doctor's absolute absence. The Bradley method is a very strict natural childbirth program. Patients will go to the hospital for the birth, but that doesn't mean they are going to let the doctor see them. The doctor will knock on the closed labor room door, and the husband will crack it open and peruse the doctor like he's some thug, or worse yet, a magazine subscription salesman. The doctor will ask to come in and they'll say "No. Everything's O.K." and slam the door. Then they probably turn to their spouse and harrumph about the damn doctors who think they run the place. They are at the hospital only on the chance something might go wrong, but if they could, they would love to keep the doctor away until the baby is born. Then they could ding a little bell, like a short order cook uses, to let the waiter know that an order is up. Bing! "Baby's done. You can come in now."

If you really want to keep your doctor away, you might employ the Laboyer Method. Among their suggestions is the delivery of the baby into a warm bath. One couple had the room kept dark. Incense was lit, and a friend was playing the lute. They were naked. All of them. The woman, her husband and the lute player. The doctor didn't want to go in. He figured he'd have to take off his clothes too.

If you are going to bother having a doctor, you might as well use his services. Remember that you are paying the doctor for his experience and advice. Well, your insurance company is paying your doctor for that, but you're paying your insurance company. O.K., most likely your employer is paying your insurance company . . . we're getting off the point. Anyway, I think the best example of a good relationship between doctor and patient can be seen in the case of a woman who was eight months pregnant and developing pre-eclampsia, a potentially dangerous condition of high blood pressure. The patient was meeting with the doctor for the third time in two weeks to discuss how this affected her birth plan. She brought along a legal pad full of questions and a husband with seemingly little interest in going over any of those questions. The doctor was very patient in answering the questions and explaining the options and how the pre-eclampsia would alter the chances for a natural delivery. The doctor sensed he wasn't satisfying the woman's concerns. She didn't want to let go of her plan. The doctor took another tack. He turned to the husband and asked, "Do you have any questions?" The husband continued to sit with eyes glazed over for a few seconds and then awoke to ask the doctor, "Doc, where did you go to med school?" Confused, the doctor responded, pointing to his diploma on the wall, "the University of Michigan." The husband then turned to his wife and asked her, "And where did you go to medical school?" He knew the answer, but she said it anyway: "I didn't." "Then why don't you just listen to the doctor?" cried the husband. There's a novel plan.

Dueling Doulas

In general, it is helpful for a woman in labor to have some support. Not just for her legs, although let's not discount the importance of that. What I'm referring to is emotional comforting. This is going to be a traumatic event, and it can be beneficial to have someone on hand who can bond with the woman going through the travails of labor. While advantageous for all types of deliveries, this is especially true for women attempting to deliver naturally. As opposed to those willing to use artificial flavoring. Some women like having their husband be that rock of support. Other women garner no benefit from having "the-bastard-who-got-me-in-this-condition" cooing words of encouragement while she grimaces in the agony of labor. (There is something to be said for the old days, when men paced the waiting room during labor.) Whether there is a significant other willing to assist the laboring mom or not, one can always buy the services of a professional labor supporter/encourager/coach/empathizer, more easily found in the yellow pages under the term "doula."

Doula is derived from the Latin "doular," meaning friendly female drill sergeant. That is essentially what they are. Add the word "up" after every time a doula says push, and you'd think you were in the Army. "Just one more push . . . up . . . come on . . . " They get right in the birth mother's face and get her to focus past the pain to the wonder of childbirth and the even greater wonder of what the hell that doula had for lunch. They cajole, tease, coax, taunt, whatever it takes to get that baby delivered and to keep the patient away from the epidural that now seems so tempting.

I have never had the misfortune of having to go to a drug rehab center, but if they don't have doulas there, they sure could use them. Give every addicted patient their own doula, and they'd be drug-free within a week. The only side effect would be that they would suffer from lifelong D.T.s—Doula Tremors. Personally, I was thinking of hiring one to stand by my refrigerator and help me fend off my food weakness.

Doulas can be helpful even if the mother takes an epidural, but you're not fully using your doula if you take the drugs. The purpose of the doula was not lost on one group of teen mothers. The pregnant girls entered a program to help with teen pregnancies. They were assigned doulas, told that doula means "helper," and assured that these woman understand what labor is like. After the program had been in place for a while, the newly pregnant had a chance to talk with the girls who had recently given birth. The newcomers quickly figured out that doulas were opposed to anesthesia, prompting them to demand, "I don't want a doula. I want an epidula."

The important thing to remember: if you hire a doula, you can fire her. Or ignore her. No first-time mom can predict how she will feel during labor, and just because some woman is in your face imploring you to keep going, doesn't mean you have to. I mean, you do have to keep going, but you can take an epidural. Or if it's too late for that, you can tell the doula to leave.

That's what a woman in El Salvador did. Doulas are common there, as are home deliveries. Her house was filled with family and friends awaiting the new arrival. Several helpful relatives were in the bedroom ready to assist. The doula had a gruff manner and was getting so annoying with her blandishments that the expectant mother snapped. She sat up, got out of bed and cold-cocked the doula with a strong right to the cheek. The doula went sprawling. The mother then cleared everyone out of her house, climbed back into bed and calmly delivered her baby with no help.

For all those patients who have wanted to punch their doula, that story was for you. And, though I don't discount the help a doula can offer, what could be more beneficial for a woman in labor than being able to punch someone in the face? In fact, I think that would be the best service a doula could provide. A laboring woman in pain would be asked, "Do you want the epidural, or would you just like to punch a doula?"

Hystericalectomy

Where doulas provide a service for laboring patients, other OB/GYN procedures have few support options. In fact, there are none. Other than those drugs. A good general anesthesia is usually sufficient to numb the brain to the surgical incisions of a hysterectomy, for example. One patient, however, felt she needed more. Although she wouldn't feel the scalpel, she felt her psyche might still be wounded, and therefore asked her psychiatrist to remain by her side during the operation. He agreed.

The psychiatrist stood alongside the operating table and comforted his patient as the general anesthesia took effect. Once she was out, so was he. He saw no reason to stay for the couple of hours of surgery. He went and had lunch. She was in a deep sleep, he was in a deep pastrami sandwich. He read the paper, made some phone calls and came back three hours later to reassure his fragile charge just as she was beginning to arouse.

Some psychiatrist try to get patients in touch with their unconscious. Now I know why. If they get there, the doctor can take a nice long lunch.

How Did That Get There?

With all this talk about agonies of childbirth, I would be remiss not to mention that some women experience very little pain or discomfort during labor. Some women are so insensate to the ordeal of pregnancy that they have the baby without even knowing it. Unbelievable, you scoff. Hey, I've seen it in the *Enquirer*. There are stories in there a couple of times a year about women who deliver into their pants or go to the bathroom and a baby comes out. These are women who claim to have had no idea they were pregnant.

Karen always gets a big kick out of these tabloid stories. Elvis sightings and space aliens have legitimate plausibility compared to a woman not knowing she was pregnant. She incredulously dismisses any such story with a curt "Come on! How could she possibly not know?"

When you think about it, pregnancy would be a tough thing to not be aware of. It's not like not knowing you were ugly. Who wants to talk about your being ugly? No one. Yet strangers will engage pregnant women in conversations. In fact, there are a lot of hints, aside from your body, that can tip you off to the fact that you're pregnant. With apologies to Jeff Foxworthy:

- If people are giving up their seat on the bus to you . . . you may be pregnant.
- If you find yourself being sent to the front of the bank line . . . you may be pregnant.
- If people keep asking, "What are you having?" and you're not in a restaurant . . . you may be pregnant.
- If you had intercourse with a male in the last several

months . . . you may be pregnant.

That last indication of pregnancy is usually the cause for feigned ignorance of one's own gestational condition. The women who claim not to know they are with child are often trying to hide the fact that they had sex. Usually it's teenagers who are trying to hide it. That it can be hidden is not a well-thought-out plan, but then one must realize that the plan is being hatched by kids whose thought process is clouded by the fact that they are . . . TEENAGERS! Many teenagers don't talk to Mom and Dad anyway, so they figure, why mention a little thing like a baby. Just get some oversized clothing, and in nine months disappear for a week, give the baby up for adoption and the 'rents will never know. There is no "Plan B."

While there may not be an official "Plan B," one generally goes into effect late in the pregnancy. It's the Political Scandal Plan—deny everything. Much like in politics, there comes a point when the denials seem supercilious, and soon after just super silly. That doesn't mean it's time to tell the truth. Keep denying.

That's the strategy one teen took to the very end. The sixteen year old was brought in to the ER by her mother. She was complaining of abdominal pain. A resident asked the girl if she might be pregnant, a suggestion the girl adamantly refuted, saying that would be "completely impossible!"

Her mother cajoled her. "Now would be the time to tell the truth." Again the daughter was adamant as to the impossibility of her being pregnant. The resident then told her that to do a full exam, he needed for her pants to come off. The patient became hysterical. The doctors tried to pull her pants off but couldn't. The patient started screaming and rolling around on the bed, and the doctors decided to cut her pants off. With the last snip as her pants came off a baby fell onto the table. The patient took one look at the baby and then looked at her mother and said, "I don't know where that came from. I am not pregnant."

How To Look Good During Delivery

One of the cruelties of giving birth is that it's hard to look good doing it. Not that there aren't women who try. I've heard of women who make themselves up after their water breaks before going into the hospital. These women have seen too many deliveries on TV and not enough in real life. Your hospital does not provide a makeup crew, so get over it. By the way, at nine months you're not skinny.

Not that I don't appreciate the attention women pay to their own beauty. My wife spends a great deal of time on her hair, and I think it looks great. I'm not always right to compliment her on it, however. Some days her hair looks fine to me, even when she feels it's not working. If I should compliment her on one of those days, she gets quite annoyed and tells me that it's not working. I guess her hair is on vacation. It's hard for me to tell if hair is working or on vacation, because my hair doesn't take vacations. If my hair doesn't want to work, it just gets up and leaves. Most of my hair is on an extended sabbatical.

Men come into the delivery room wearing whatever they had on when their wives' labor began. Women have carefully picked out the outfit they want to wear to the hospital. They've taken the time to check themselves in the mirror, even doing that little turn in the mirror to check themselves from behind. Dare I suggest that no man does this. When we get dressed, we look to see what the result is head on, if at all. Who cares what we look like from behind? We could be naked back there for all we know. We could be wearing paper doll

111

cutout clothing and wouldn't know it because we don't check from behind. That's probably why men came up with the expression "Better cover your ass." It's a reminder.

I did labor in jeans and a T-shirt. That's the outfit I'm most confident in. My wife had enough on her mind; she didn't need to worry about matching something for me. I'm getting better at picking things out for myself. I went to "Color-Me-Beautiful." It's a consulting company that tells you what colors you look good in based on what "season" you are. I'm an Autumn, which means I look good in . . . October and November, I guess. I think I peak near Thanksgiving. The colors are spectacular, but of course, you can't get near me with all the tourists.

No matter how much women know about all that beauty stuff, there is only one way to look sensational during the birth of your child. Have a surrogate. If it's not quite that important to you, you can take heart in knowing that you will probably look better than a woman we'll call Tracy.

Tracy was a young mother of a one-year-old when she went into labor with child number two in the middle of the night. Unaware of the hospital policy prohibiting infants from delivery rooms, she brought along the one-year-old and her husband. Second babies generally come faster than first ones, and when she got to the hospital she found that she was nine centimeters dilated. She became quite upset when told that her existing child had to leave, which meant that her husband also had to leave. He vowed to quickly find a babysitter and return immediately. Tracy was now in a panic. She doubted her husband could make it back in time. She tried to get herself under control with some deep breaths, but her nervousness caused the breaths to come faster than she intended. Tracy started to hyperventilate.

Hyperventilating can cause you to pass out, and when you are unconscious it's really hard to get you to push. The way to get a person to stop hyperventilating is to get them to breathe more carbon dioxide. This is most easily done by having the hyperventilator breathe into a paper bag. A nurse who had brought her lunch happened to have one handy. It was a small bag, however, and Tracy couldn't hold it on herself, as the hyperventilating had started to cause her arms and legs to contract and spasm. The nurses didn't have an extra pair of hands. With all the million dollars' worth of equipment in a hospital, no one has yet to invent a paper bag face holder-oner. That's the problem with modern medicine. The quick-thinking nurses found a larger grocery paper bag and put it over Tracy's head. (More than the environment can be saved by choosing paper over plastic at the checkout counter.)

So there Tracy was, arms flailing, paper bag over her head, when her doctor arrived for the delivery. The doctor's first thought was that she had a patient who was in the witness-protection program. Then the nurses explained the reason for the bag. The OB felt that delivering like that was too degrading, but under the circumstances it was necessary. She did the only thing she could to help—take a magic marker and draw a face on the front of the bag. It was like that when Tracy's child was born. Her husband never made it back.

Would you believe me if I told you that kid grew up to become the Unknown Comic? No? Well, how about just a die-hard Cubs fan?

Fashion Show

You work hard to get your degree. You have an important job. You can afford the finest clothes. Now that you're a doctor, what do you get to wear? Scrubs. Oh, the injustice of it all! Everyone wearing the same thing. All those egos squelched by an inability to make their fashion statement. You might as well be working at Burger King.

Scrubs are very egalitarian. Since everyone wears them, you usually have to look on their hospital badge to know a nurse from a doctor. At one time there may have been a color hierarchy, but that all came out in the wash. Laundry was the great equalizer. Once lights and darks commingled, societal barriers begin to break down. That might be a quote from Abraham Lincoln, I don't know. I do know that there are some interesting scrub colors. (Read the following with a haughty French accent as the doctors sashay down the runway. Come on, you can do it.) Zis year, zee hottest new color for zee sexiest doctors eez faded puke green. Eet makes zee bold statement: illness eez all around me. Ooo la la! (O.K., *finito* with the French.)

Aside from being egalitarian, scrubs are utilitarian. They could also well be Unitarian, but I wouldn't recommend you wear them to church. Having a color palette that covers the entire spectrum of bodily fluids that are likely to soil them, the scrubs look clean much longer than normal clothes. They also are very functional in terms of size. They come in two sizes—huge and Spruce Goose. Most scrubs can fit a small nation in the pants. Certainly one of those tiny European countries near Monaco. They have a long drawstring at the waist that enables anyone smaller than a Dick Gregory sympathy case to wear it.

The scrubs ensemble would not be complete without matching shoes and hat. The shoe covers are like a large baggie. (For all I know they may be ziplocked. That would explain the green color. It's how hospital workers know they're sealed.) The hats are rejects from ladies' curling sets. The full scrub is the most unattractive attire known to man. There isn't a person alive who could look good wearing it. Claudia Schiffer wouldn't get a second glance in the full scrub. If soap opera doctors wore the full scrub, *General Hospital* would have been canceled after one week.

Like the L.A.P.D., the scrub is designed to protect and serve. On occasion it has failed in its mission. One very nearsighted doctor was known to get quite close to suture episiotomies. In one instance he finished and stood up, but his hat didn't come with him. He had sewn it into the episiotomy. He obviously knew that it is proper for a gentleman to remove his hat in the presence of a lady.

Some people have tried to accessorize the full scrub. I have seen hospital workers with pant legs tucked into knee socks. It does add a hint of sexy intrigue, much like leg warmers, and it makes you wonder if perhaps this nurse might just go flashdance on her coffee break. The other hint of intrigue comes in wondering why anyone would want to ruin a good pair of socks.

In my opinion, the only truly perfect accessory for the full scrub is a jacket. A lab coat to be exact. Still a badge of honor for physicians, for me it doesn't carry the panache it once did. When I know that there are also guys in a lab coats testing whether the new Fruity Pebbles are really fruitier or just slightly more scrumpdillyicious, it takes away from the mystique.

Karen has a lab coat. She has several. Not understanding

fashion, I don't know why she has more than one. I guess each one serves a different function. There's one for casual doctoring, one for formal deliveries, and one for just weekend doctoring around the house. That's also known as the "My husband won't turn up the thermostat" coat.

I don't know how she comes by these coats or why they multiply. Since only doctors or scientists are meant to wear them, there must be some kind of control center that doles them out. As far as I am aware, there is no white lab coat store. I couldn't wear one even if I found such a store. You need to have the confidence and comfort of having lots of degrees to carry off the lab coat with style. The full scrub and lab coat is not an inbred trait. It's probably taught in med school and then ingrained through hands-on experience during residency. One such experience was Dr. Carl's.

Carl was a good ole Texan. Tall and lanky, he was most comfortable in his jeans and cowboy boots. That was how he was dressed on his first night on-call as a resident. Dr. Carl didn't know where the scrubs were kept, but he figured he'd have time to get his bearings straight later. It was a quiet night. There was only one patient on the board, and she was in very early labor. So first thing he wanted to do was get comfortable in his call room. That's what he was doing when a nurse yelled out that they needed him STAT!

The early-laboring patient was having major complications and needed a crash C-section. Crash means immediately, and Dr. Carl wasn't even in his scrubs. He quickly stripped and found the scrubs in a cabinet. It wasn't the regular pants-and-shirt set that he found, it was the nurse's tunic. He had no choice. He threw it on, pulled his boots back on and ran to the operating room. There he performed a successful C-section in a dress that didn't quite cover his bony knees, black socks and cowboy boots. The clothes didn't make the man. They made the man a woman.

Leggo My Leg Oh

A woman comes into the emergency room in labor. She is quickly sent up to labor and delivery, where they check to find that she is complete and ready to push. There is rushing all around. Residents and nurses come to assist. The woman starts pushing, but something doesn't feel right. As the residents and nurses all yell at her to PUSH! she stops and says, "Wait! I think I could do much better if I take off my leg."

The shocked physicians and nurses all stop. They watch as she removes her artificial leg and then delivers her baby in two more pushes.

She re-attaches her leg before driving home.

The Poop Deck

For those of you who haven't been through labor, consider this fair warning—a baby is usually not the only thing that comes out of your body during delivery. Delivery requires a great deal of pushing and grunting, and there are other orifices in close proximity and, well—how best to delicately put this?—shit happens. There is no need to be embarrassed by this, however. The doctor and nurses have all seen this many times before. Sometimes they even encourage it, so that a woman won't restrain herself in pushing out the baby. Everyone is prepared for it. Usually.

One pushing patient kept telling the doctor that she "had to go" over and over again. The doctor told her that it was O.K. She shouldn't worry about it. Just go ahead and go. The doctor was expecting the usual bowel movement, when the patient let out a huge stream of urine that arced through the air and soaked the doctor. That's gotta be worse than having a waiter spill coffee on you.

Other women are more nonchalant about relieving themselves. Or more likely, they don't even realize what they've done with all the pushing. Since it's such a common thing, the doctor and nurses don't even mention it. The next situation, though, was pretty rare. One woman pushed so hard that her two front teeth came flying out of her mouth. They were false teeth, so it's not like she was pushing that hard, but even with false teeth, the effort was there. The teeth flew out of her mouth and landed . . . yep, right in her own deposit. A nurse quickly retrieved the teeth and was going to clean them off, but before she could the patient yelled, "I need my teeth!" Or, more accurately, "I eed my eef." She grabbed the teeth out of the nurse's hand and put them back in her mouth. I'll say it with you. Ewww!

It isn't only patients who find the need to relieve themselves during labor. A doctor may get the urge, too, and that can radically alter your birth experience. One first-year resident had a bit of stomach upset when the head of the department showed up to lead rounds that morning. Despite his respect for the prestigious faculty member, the first year couldn't stifle the gas that had built up. He let a fart loose just as the group of doctors entered a laboring patient's room. The resident had managed to control the sound, but the smell was immediate. The chief took one whiff and said, "Do you smell that? This patient needs a C-section immediately! That smell clearly indicates she is infected." The terrified first-year could not dare to correct his superior, and the most unnecessary C-section in history was performed.

Although it's unusual for someone else's stomach trouble to affect your labor, it can be hard to distinguish the pain of labor from the pain of intestinal upset. At least as a man, this is what I like to believe. If you tell me that labor hurts like I've-been-cavalier-about-eating-shawarma-from-street-vendors-in-poor-sections-of-Cairo, then I feel your pain. I'm assuming that labor pain has some similar characteristics, because it is in the same general midsection area, and because some women have made the mistake of confusing the two. None has made the mistake so dramatically as a woman who came into the hospital prepared to deliver her first child.

The woman showed up at the emergency room nearly nine months pregnant and doubled over in pain. Seeing a pregnant woman will send an emergency room into panic. Gunshot wounds, a guy with swords sticking out of his back, Ebola virus—these things are routinely handled with alacrity and vigor in a big-city emergency room. But a pregnant woman?

"Get her up to labor and delivery, STAT! Who knows what horrible things could happen? Let the OBs do their voodoo." So the woman was quickly whisked upstairs, where the OB residents got her into a birthing room and checked her. She was barely one centimeter dilated. And the contractions were quite irregular. The doctor thought this might not be labor but stomach trouble, and he gave her an enema. Moments later the woman leapt off her bed and ran to the bathroom, where she "delivered" a five-pound, four-ounce wonder. The doctor described it as a Duraflame log. He saw it because it would not flush down the toilet, it was so big. They had to call maintenance to take care of it. The maintenance guy came up, took a look and mumbled something about this being a job for a team that would come in the morning. Then he simply put some yellow tape across the bathroom door as if it were a crime scene. But not before the crime scene photographer took a Polaroid of the offense. That picture is proudly posted on the bulletin board among all the pictures of babies born on the floor.

Macho Man

I don't know what a woman thinks about in the moments during and immediately after giving birth. I imagine there is a wide range of emotions that are traversed in those sacred minutes. Memories of the past, hopes for the future, the physical extremes of the present all collide. Fear, joy, relief, love. I'm just guessing.

And there beside you, if you're lucky, the man who shares in this miracle. What is he thinking about? The shared life that you have brought into the world? The same fear and joy and relief and love that has sent you to tears?

No. He's thinking about sex.

Not the whole time, mind you. But, somewhere in the middle of sharing all those emotions, the same thought arises in every man's head, "I hope there's not too much ripping and damage, because I was kind of hoping to use that again."

Selfish, yes. But also practical. Your partner is taking a long-term view. He realizes that although sex is the last thing on your mind at this moment, at some point in the next decade, you will want to have sex again, even if in your current state you swear it won't be with him. He just wants to make sure there's a possibility. For your sake.

The delicate part at that moment is that the man use discretion in conveying his concerns. This is all the more important if the doctor is a woman. She may not fully understand that a man only has his wife's best interests in mind. Like if your doctor is Karen, for example.

More than once, Karen has been in the process of sewing

up the episiotomy when the husband will pipe in with a smirk, "Put in an extra stitch for me." To which my wife always answers, "Why? Are you so small that she couldn't feel it before?" Proving that men aren't the only ones who can be crude.

Women, in fact, do become quite unladylike when the pushing begins. The swearing during labor is only a precursor to the macho gamesmanship that comes with the episiotomy. While the man is asking for another stitch to increase his pleasure, the woman will ask for an extra so she can say she had more than her best friend. She is preparing to one-up her friends' war stories.

WOMAN 1: I pushed for seven hours and then had a third-degree tear. Twelve stitches!

WOMAN 2: Well, I labored for two days, and just as they were going to take me back for a C-section, I pushed that baby out. Had to have 22 stitches!

WOMAN 3: I was three weeks past my due date and had a ten-and-a-half pounder! Needed 83 stitches in the episiotomy!

WOMAN 4: I gave birth to a full-size adult. Had to split myself in two like a cyborg. They put me back together with super glue and rivets.

WOMEN 1, 2 AND 3: Big deal. No stitches.

This game is complete bluster on the part of Karen's patients. Karen never counts the number of stitches she uses. Neither do any of her colleagues, as far as she knows. The episiotomy is sewn in one long thread and then tied at the end. Not stitch by stitch. These women will have to find something else to brag about. Length of string used, perhaps. Alternatively, length of labor, weeks past the due date, and insensitivity of your partner are all options.

The last option is the easiest for one-upmanship. Most men will offer support and encouragement and stay by their wife's side depending, of course, on what major sporting event might be happening at the same time. Don't forget that it wasn't until a few years ago that the father was even allowed in the delivery room, so current generations have a genetic lack of interest in the birth process. Men know that all they can do is wait, so they prefer to wait playing cards. If that means bringing some friends into the delivery room, so be it.

That camaraderie can go against hospital policy. For most women, i.e., those who don't have their deliveries broadcast over the Internet, privacy is valued. A birth is to be shared by the mother and father alone. But that assumes a traditional relationship. What policy does one have for the woman who had four men attending to her during labor? The doctor walked in prepared to deliver and had to decide which man was to be allowed to stay.

"Who are these men?" he asked

The woman was completely clear in delineating her relationship with each man. "That's my husband, that's the father of the baby, that's my boyfriend, and that's my man."

The doctor shooed out all but the father of the baby because, as we know, it takes a village to raise a child, not to deliver one. It's just extremely heartening to know that for every mother abandoned to deliver on her own, there are four guys attending to one other delivery somewhere. Who said men have trouble with commitment?

O.K. Everybody says it. That doesn't mean most men don't overcome the fear. While some men may overcome the fear of commitment to one woman, they may transfer the fear of commitment to the child. Others may be willing to father and even be a father to many children while remaining unable to devote themselves to one woman. Even so, they might show up to a delivery as a matter of duty. Caught up in the emotion of the moment, they may slip and reveal a rare desire for fealty, expressing adoration for the woman beyond her sexual enchantments. That had to be what happened to the gentleman who watched as the mother of his four children was being wheeled back to deliver his fifth. In a brief second of indiscretion he yelled, "Now, y'all take care of her because I love her and I'm going to marry her someday."

Thankfully, he didn't add, "And put in an extra stitch for me."

Revenge of the Placenta

Pity the poor placenta. After sustaining a new life for nine months, it is expelled with complete indifference while the child it supported is given all the attention and adulation. Well, not always. Some people eat the placenta. I don't know why. I guess they figure delivering a baby is hard work, they should at least get a meal out of it. For them the placenta is the uterus' way of saying, "Would you like fries with that?"

As far as I know, frying is the most common preparation of the placenta. I don't have any good recipes, but if you plan on serving it at a party I would recommend lots of ketchup. The people who do eat the placenta are generally into natural birth and other things natural, so it would seem problematic for a vegetarian, but then no one was killed in getting the placenta, so it could be O.K. I'm not certain. I would consult a vegetarian clergyman. Speaking of which, I would almost bet it's not Kosher. Certainly, if the mother isn't Jewish.

Those who don't eat it ignore it. There is no excitement or urgent yells of "PUSH" to have the mother get the placenta out. It usually comes without much effort. On occasion, however, the placenta doesn't want to come out, and the patient is given a drug called methergine, which makes the uterus contract. At the same time, the doctor or nurse will push on the uterus to help the placenta come out.

That's what a doctor was doing while an intern waited between the patient's legs for signs of the reluctant placenta. The combination of the drug and the pushing was more than was necessary. With one push the placenta flew out of the woman and landed with a splat right on the intern's face. It stuck there like a cream pie in a Three Stooges melee. The intern passed out. The placentas had their one shining moment.

Lucky Charms

My research shows that women have been giving birth for well over a century now. I guess they had been doing it long before that, but it was different back then. The birthing experience has changed. No longer do women slip away to the field in the middle of the night to get their epidural. Most babies are born in hospitals. Modern science and hospital deliveries are reportedly two reasons for a lowered infant mortality rate and a lower mortality rate of birthing mothers. That's the good news. The bad news: insurance doesn't cover parking. The trade-off seems worth it, but other things have been lost.

Ancient cultures had their own traditions, rituals and superstitions associated with birth. In some parts of central Asia, whole villages did a circle dance around the mother. Certain tribal groups believed that the placenta has special powers, so the day after the birth it was served as a feast for the whole tribe. A Jewish custom is to eat a corned beef sandwich on rye. It has nothing to do with giving birth, but compared to eating the placenta it seems like such a sensible custom. These rich cultural rituals have mostly disappeared in the modern American hospital, and I think we are a little poorer for it.

That's not to say that there aren't superstitions that have survived. Medical science hasn't completely eliminated the uncertainties of childbirth. People pray for healthy babies, for uncomplicated deliveries, for boys or girls. And they don't just pray, they think they have the means to bring it about.

Usually it's just a matter of wearing the right pair of lucky underwear.

I find it a bit silly that some people wear lucky clothing to a birth. Personally, I could never rationalize that what I was wearing had any affect on something so divine as the birth of my child. In my view, lucky underwear only has power over my sports teams. When I'm wearing my lucky underwear, I know they are going to win. Unfortunately, I only have one pair of lucky underwear, which is why my teams rarely have a long winning streak. After a few days, hygiene begins to outweigh victory. Plus, even though I do it, deep down I know my underwear doesn't matter. If it did, then the other team's strategy would be to get my underwear. Opposing-team coaches and television analysts would be diagramming where I'm ticklish and where I'm most vulnerable to a sneak pantsing. That hasn't happened yet.

Yet superstitions are very real to those who believe them. The most common one in hospitals is the effect of the full moon. Some nurses will swear that there are more deliveries during the full moon. Others confess that, although there is no statistical proof of more deliveries during a full moon, the ones that happen have more complications. Personally, I think the logic behind the myth is that things do get randomly crazy, but the only time it's noted is when the craziness happens to coincide with a full moon. Also, during a full moon there tends to be an increase in the number of werewolves.

If the full moon theory were true, hospital workers would be consulting the lunar calendar before they made out their monthly schedule. And weathermen would be giving tide information on their "exclusive forecast." (How do these stations tout exclusive forecasts? Like no one else knows rain is coming?) It doesn't happen. That debunks that.

Myths abound about another aspect of pregnancy—the sex of the baby. We've all heard that how a mother carries the fetus is a predictor of the baby's sex. If it sits more out front, it's a boy; if the woman is spreading at the hips, it's a girl. There is also the pencil method. You tie a pencil on a string and drop it in front of the baby. If the pencil comes to rest in an up and down position it's a boy, if it spins in a circle it's a girl. Then there is the urine test. Before flushing, a woman can pour Drano into the toilet on top of her urine. If it turns pink, it's a girl; bluish-brown, it's a boy. If the Drano doesn't turn any color you'll have to call the Roto-Rooter man to come and determine the sex of your baby.

All these indicators have about as much validity as the gambling tip line that offers the winners "GUARANTEED." The only thing that's guaranteed is that they'll be right fifty percent of the time. I could start a business with the come-on, "The sex of your baby—guaranteed or your money back." So what if I only get to keep half the money. There's a sucker born every minute, and for a couple of bucks I'll gladly tell you if you have a boy sucker or a girl sucker.

Doctors are also susceptible to superstition. Their favorite ones surround household remedies for inducing labor in over-due mothers. Desperate mothers tired of carrying what seems to be a cannonball in their belly seek out "natural" remedies. The most natural one being—call your doctor and beg for an induction. Most doctors refuse to induce patients solely on the basis that the patient is tired of being pregnant. Often they won't induce even on the condition that the patient is tired of being pregnant and has a gun. Instead they will suggest things. Things like drinking mother's milk or castor oil or castor oil with O.J. (The drink, not the guy.) Of those, only the mother's milk has some scientific basis. Mother's milk naturally has pitocin in it and can potentially help induce labor, but there is no guarantee in any of these. The main reason your doctor prescribes these remedies? Whether you decide to chase down a nursing woman who is willing to give you her breast milk or you spend hours on the toilet from taking castor oil, you are going to be too busy to bother the doctor for a while.

The most common recommendation to induce labor is to have sex. I believe this also is another veiled attempt by the doctor to get the patient out of his hair. At 40 weeks, most women are so repulsed by the idea of sex that the mere suggestion would send them running from the person who brought it up. But maybe it really works. I don't know what the scientific basis could be. Maybe the baby feels like someone's knocking and he should open up the door. Some believe there is something in the sperm. In any case, doctors should make certain the patient understands that sex here means the presidential definition of sex, i.e., intercourse. That wasn't clear to a woman who was being sent home from the hospital for false labor. This had happened a couple of times over the last few days and the woman was distraught. She pleaded, "Is there anything else I can do to help this along?" The doctor nonchalantly replied on his way out of the room, "All you need is a good dose of sperm." The second he left, the patient burst into tears. The nurse who remained in the room tried to console her by telling her that it's not uncommon for women to be sent home several times before real labor starts. "It's not that," the patient replied, "It's just that, well, I've never swallowed before."

Slippery Suckers

During a normal delivery, the most valuable service you get from your doctor and the hospital support staff is the cleaning service. I'm not talking about the sheets, although thank goodness you don't have to try to salvage those for company. I'm talking about the baby cleaning. When the doctor or a nurse first hands you your fresh bundle of joy, it comes as a neatly wrapped package: a dry baby in a blanket with a little hat on. Somehow, a miraculous fifteen seconds after the cord has been cut, the kid is showered, shaved and sent to the haberdasher. Be glad this is done, otherwise it is unlikely you would be able to hold your own baby. When they first come out, babies are as slippery as a greased watermelon in the swimming hole. (Greased watermelon in the swimming hole also happens to be another term for the placenta.)

There are only two people who can handle a slick newborn as it slides out of the mother—a highly trained doctor or midwife, or a soft-handed, gold-glove shortstop. Most people go with the doctor only because they are less likely to become a free agent. You know those shortstops; they're all set to catch your baby, but the second Steinbrenner offers a bigger baby they jump ship. So most people go with the traditional baby-catching professional.

Don't think the pros are infallible as receivers, however. They do drop them on occasion. It's not good to drop a baby. Recovery is tough. What can you say? Well, the doctor can't really say anything and look good. The only hope is that a quick-thinking nurse comes up with a line to cover. I have only heard of two that are worth repeating. In one instance the nurse simply continued describing the action the doctor was taking in a very calm voice as if it were all part of the plan. " . . . And now the doctor is going to take the baby out of the birthing bucket . . . ."

The other quick rebound was by a nurse who informed the mother that, "Usually we have to drop them two or three times to get them to cry." What a lucky mother, to have a child already ahead of the curve at birth!

Beyond the Call of Duty

Nobody wants an emergency when they go to the hospital, but you'd like to think that your doctor could wisely handle any complication. All doctors are trained for difficult situations, yet there are only a few special physicians who show a commitment and effort that goes way beyond the normal call of duty. Whether it's during labor or surgery, the following OBs fought through their own pain to help their patient. We salute them.

Doctor George was in the middle of an intricate laperoscopy. The laperscope is a fine laser which enables doctors to perform procedures without cutting the patient open. Part way into the surgery, George began to feel excruciating pain in his side. He knew what it was. He was passing a kidney stone. Unfortunately, there was no one qualified to immediately take over the surgery. George knew he had to push through, but the pain was terrible. He couldn't take a narcotic and still perform the surgery, so he opted for a non-narcotic pain reliever called Toredol. The fastest way to get the Toredol working? An injection. So, without stopping the surgery George had a nurse pull down his pants and give him a shot in his butt.

The rigors of surgery can't compare to the physical demands of delivering a baby. And I'm talking about the doctor. It was only a few years ago that most hospitals had separate labor and delivery rooms. When the time came, the patient was wheeled from one room to another. If the patient had an epidural rendering her legs numb and useless, she had

133

to be lifted over to the birthing table. This was what Doctor T. was doing when he pulled something in his groin. The pain was sharp and strong, but with the impending delivery, the doctor had to overlook it. After a few moments, the pain went away and he could concentrate on the delivery, which went very well.

After the baby was born, Doctor T. sent the husband down to tell the rest of the family that they could come up to see the baby. He then sat down to sew up the episiotomy. As he was sewing, the pain returned. This time it was worse, and he started to have a vaso-vegal reaction, which I don't understand either, except that it meant he was going to pass out. Now, there are better places to pass out than between a woman's legs after a delivery. There is a bucket kept there that collects the blood, placenta and various fluids from the birth. Doctor T.'s head fell forward right into that bucket. With his head down, the blood came rushing back, and he immediately regained consciousness. He lifted his head up, only to become faint again and fall back into the bucket.

By this time, there was near panic in the delivery room. The nurses weren't sure if the doctor had had a heart attack. They called for help. Soon the doctor was able to speak, but one nurse felt he should keep his head down, and every time he tried to get up she would push his head back down into the bucket. Amid near pandemonium, help arrived, and Doctor T. was lifted onto a gurney and wheeled out of the room. On the way out, he passed the baby's father, along with the extended family. A look of panic overtook the father when he saw the doctor being wheeled past. Only the worst could have run through his mind as he frantically yelled, "What happened to the doctor?"

The gurney continued on to the elevators to take the stricken physician upstairs for examination. The elevator doors opened, and out walked the Lamaze tour, conducted to give students a comfort level with the labor and delivery floor.

Several members of the class recognized their doctor as he was being hustled onto the elevator. "Is that my doctor?" one of them asked the tour guide. "I'm sure it's nothing," reassured the guide. Then he went right back into his standard patter. "Being up here should put you at ease with the whole delivery process."

The Worst Place To Have A Baby?

In researching this book, I heard about some horrible delivery experiences and I made it my business to find the worst possible birthing circumstance for a pregnant woman. After much careful research, I determined that the worst possible place to have a baby would be on the Titanic. There would be so much commotion, no one would pay any attention to you. Although, the advantage would be that you would have no trouble getting ice chips. Since giving birth on the Titanic is no longer possible, I concluded that the worst place on land must be a war zone. Most authors wouldn't travel to a war zone just for one measly chapter. I wouldn't either. I was, however, willing to talk to an OB who was in El Salvador in the mid-80's.

Dr. John (not the musician) was in El Salvador because he was a Catholic priest. He subsequently became an OB/GYN and now brags about performing the triple play for his parishioners: He can marry them, deliver their baby, and baptize it. And if you sign up for the first two, the baptism is free. At the time he was in El Salvador Dr. John didn't know that much about obstetrics. He found himself in a rural part of the country, assisting in deliveries that were managed by two 80-year-old midwives. There were no doctors left in the area. The educated elite had fled from the civil war. The younger midwives had escaped to the city, where they could make better money. Only these two fixtures remained. One of the two was losing her eyesight. She was the one you wanted, because the other one was an alcoholic. Her fee for a delivery was $1.50 for a baby girl and $3.50 for a baby boy. That, and a case of beer. The beer had to be a down payment, waiting for her upon arrival. Sustenance for the arduous labor she was about to witness.

If you weren't enthralled with the aged midwives, you could try to make it to the hospital. That required even more money for "El Supremo"— the four-wheel-drive truck that could get you there. You needed a good vehicle, both because of the rough roads and the fact that you might need to outmaneuver a death squad or sniper fire from the guerrillas. Or you could try being inconspicuous by walking. That is what one laboring woman tried. At least until she came across a disputed roadblock. A firefight was raging around the roadblock, but the woman decided to go for it. As she was climbing over the roadblock, she got shot right in the butt. Rethinking her objective, the woman calmly turned around and went back home to deliver her baby.

Dr. John was continually amazed at the fortitude of these young Salvadoran women and their ability to deal with the pain of labor. Perhaps living in the midst of continual military activity hardens you. He watched as one patient was clearly having complications. The baby was stuck, and the nun who was attending to the woman knew she had only one chance of saving the child. The nun pulled out a pocket knife and, absent any anesthesia, performed a C-section. The patient simply gritted her teeth. Mother and baby did fine. Incredible what people will do when they have to. Incredible that a nun carries a pocket knife. Now, every time I see a nun, I assume that underneath her habit, she's packing.

Dr. John figured that their hardiness came from working in the fields and carrying water jugs on their heads. Their physical strength was evidenced by a laboring girl who pulled on a rope for leverage as she tried to push with her contractions. I don't fully understand the concept, but her doula had tied a rope around the crossbeam of the grass hut. Either the girl was stronger than anticipated or the crossbeam was weaker, because as the pain of labor increased, so did the strength of the girl's pulling. She finally broke the beam and brought the house tumbling on top of her. Poor girl. She had to combine the two most difficult tasks in a person's life—having a newborn and having to move.

Hard to believe that these strong women look up to Americans as examples of good health. It's all because of advertising. The name "Hair Bear" is popular for little babies. Dr. John wondered about the odd name. Were the babies exceptionally hairy? Is it some bastardization of teddy bear? Then he realized it was the Spanish pronunciation of Gerber. The locals all wanted their babies to look like the cherub pictured on the jar of baby food. If they didn't look like that, the girls could at least hope to grow up to look like Betty Crocker.

Dr. John's favorite delivery from his days in El Salvador was one he missed. The husband had eluded a gun battle to summon the priest to help in the delivery. The two of them rushed back through the darkness to the windowless mud hut. Too late. Mom had already delivered. The men could see the mother resting on one side of the shack, where two small flames were burning. There they saw twins lying on their backs. Camphor had been placed on their umbilical cords and lit in an effort to cauterize the bleeding. The babies' birthday suit had come with its own birthday candle. Dr. John went over, made a wish and blew the babies out.

So next time you think it's tough having a baby, imagine having to deliver twins, in a war zone in a windowless mud hut, by yourself. Of course, you're right, she didn't have to deal with insurance forms.

Insurance

Gender and experience are not the only factors in choosing a doctor. There is also insurance. The insurance industry is like a disapproving parent anxious to foil any relationship you're in.

PATIENT: Why can't I go to that doctor? I like that doctor!
INSURANCE: That doctor is no good for you. That doctor uses a hospital that our kind won't go to. I'm sorry, but you have to find someone else.
PATIENT: But, I love that doctor. I want to have babies with that doctor.
INSURANCE: Go to your room.

The whole process of choosing a plan and figuring out which doctors are accepted on which plan is mind-numbing. There are PPOs and HMOs and POSs with CNA or BCBS . . . who can keep track? My sensible solution, which I hope to get through Congress, is that you or your employer pick a plan, and then you can go to any doctor whose name can be spelled out by the letters in the plan. For Example, I'm covered by AFTRA on a PCP, so I could go to a Dr. PRAFT or a Dr. CARP or any doctor named PAT or for a gastroenterologist, a Dr. . . . well, I don't have to spell them all out for you. It's a plan that is simple and fun. Just make sure you get some vowels in your health plan.

I realize that should my plan go through, Dr. Jaffe is not going to be an easy name to conjure up. "J" is an uncommon letter on health plans, but I have confidence that Karen would still find a large patient base. She's so popular now that she is closing her practice to new patients. Word has spread. My wife gives good baby.

"We give good baby" is not her slogan, by the way. Karen doesn't have a slogan. Yet. Doctors have not reached that point where they are advertising on buses or shopping bags with cute slogans or discount coupons. I imagine that one day it will come to that. There will be "specialists of the week," and some ambitious obstetrician is going to offer "Delivery in 30 minutes or less or it's free." I hope it doesn't get that far, but just in case, I copyrighted the tag line—"We open our arms to women who spread their legs." Some practice is going to pay me big bucks for the rights to that one.

Karen would like to see everyone who wants to come to her, but then she wouldn't get to spend the time necessary with each patient. Patients would feel slighted, get angry and leave the practice. Bad word of mouth would spread, and she would lose all her patients and have to build up the practice again to get to the point where she would have to close it. So she's stopping that circle right here.

It isn't just Karen's practice that is getting busier. As insurance companies reduce reimbursements, some doctors are closing up shop, leaving fewer OBs to take care of the same patient pool. Managed care has managed to reduce the obscene amounts of money that doctors used to make and put it in the hands of the insurance companies. Now don't you feel better about health-care reform?

Any doctor will tell you that their complaint with managed care isn't the money, it's that managed care dictates patient care. How does it do that? With money. Doctors could make decisions based strictly on the well-being of the patient, but since that doesn't always pay the bills .... Let me give you an example:

Karen had a patient who had decided to have a tubal ligation. She wouldn't need her Norplant birth control anymore, so while she was under for the tubal ligation, Karen removed the Norplant. The insurance company was billed for both procedures. Karen received the standard discounted check of about $85 for the Norplant procedure, and since the tubal was a concurrent procedure and the patient was already there . . . she was paid $2.95. Two ninety-five for cutting somebody open and going into their uterus! The 95 cents kills me. Like it's retail. Psychologically, people are going to buy a lot more tubal ligations at $2.95 than at three dollars.

Practically speaking, this changes the way Karen will do things in the future. She has learned that she can't afford to do concurrent procedures. If they are done on different days, she'll get the usual and customary payment for each procedure. She knows it's a hardship on a patient to come in twice for procedures that can be done in one shot, but for the couple of dollars that she'd get paid, why do it? It's not right, but she needs to make a living. Obviously, something needs to be changed.

I suggest upfront, no-haggle pricing. Like the new approach many car dealers are taking. The insurance companies need to come on board and establish set prices that the doctors can agree to. Then let the patients know how much things cost and how much of the cost the insurance companies will pay. There can be a surgical showroom—window displays of surgical procedures and how much they cost. Doctors can charge what they want, but they should be able to explain that the reason why their hysterectomy costs more than another doctor's is that with this hysterectomy, you get cup holders. Then, if they cut you open and find further complications, they should wake you and ask if you want the extra work done and tell you how much it will be. This plan may need a little tinkering, but I haven't heard you come up with a better one.

Neither have I heard the government come up with any

good proposals. But that isn't a surprise. Personally, I hope they never get involved. The last thing we need is the government coming in to screw things up. We can screw things up just fine by ourselves, thank you. But make no mistake, even though our government doesn't run health care, their chocolate-covered handprints are all over it. Mostly these are unnecessary restrictions designed to keep science and medicine from going beyond certain ethical boundaries. Like the recently passed law against cloning humans. A good idea, but completely ineffective. What's the punishment? Imprisonment? Death? Who cares? If I make five more of me and one of them has to go to jail, so what? You want me to serve three life sentences? I'll make another three of me. The government does not think ahead.

In obstetrics, the most recent governmental intrusion involves the father's role of cutting the baby's cord at birth. This is a time-honored tradition that is now controversial for some reason. I think there may be concern that contaminated blood might come out of the cord. Or maybe there are new discrimination laws forcing delivery rooms to carry left-handed scissors. I don't know. I was only made aware of the issue one day while perusing an OB/GYN web site on the Internet.

A nurse in Atlanta worked with a physician who was no longer letting dads cut the cord because, as he understood it, he could be fined $2,000 by OSHA for that. In trying to confirm this, the nurse posted it on the web site to check the veracity of the alleged fine. A doctor, well versed in the ways of government bureaucracy, fired off this reply:

"Actually, the prohibition of cord cutting comes from the IRS. If the father is allowed to cut the cord, then he can bill the doctor for those services. Billing code CPT 59413. Once billed, (providing that the father obtained pre-certification and is on the provider list), the physician must then send an EOB requesting an operating note and thus delay payment. Once the info has been received, the physician can pay at 60-

70% of the price charged, less the withhold. In some capped plans they may arbitrarily reduce the amount paid per relative value unit. After all that, the physician must send a 1099 to the dads as independent contractors."

See? Everything was simple until that 1099, when the government had to get involved.

Hospital Policy

Big institutions like to have policies. Policies deter lawsuits. Policies allow hospitals to be in control. Policies are fun to ridicule. With the spread of body piercing in these parts to all parts, hospitals have had to institute policies on how to deal with it. Below is one hospital's policy.

The obstetrical team is to be made aware of all body piercing jewelry.

The patient will be asked to remove body piercing jewelry. Some patients will say piercing jewelry cannot be removed. If the tongue, lip or nose is pierced, anesthesia will assess the ability to maintain an airway, including the ability to intubate, should the necessity arise, and determine if the piercing jewelry must be removed. Anesthesia staff reserve the right to tell the patient and surgeon that due to the piercing jewelry, airway maintenance could be a problem. They may ask the patient to remove it, and if it cannot be removed, to cancel an elective case. In all other cases, anesthesia and the surgeon, along with the patient, will determine the course of action.

The use of an electrosurgical unit (ESU) on patients with pierced body parts may produce alternate-site tissue burns. The surgeon may select not to use the ESU.

The surgeon may choose to remove the piercing jewelry once the patient is anesthetized, and replace at the completion of the surgery. Jewelry to remain in place and not in the mouth or ears will be bandaged if such will not interfere with the surgery. This may help to prevent accidental removal or loss and may help insulate jewelry when ESU is used. Although every effort will be made to secure jewelry, the hospital is not responsible for jewelry.

Adopted by Perinatal Collaborative Management Committee. June 1997.

To put it in easy-to-understand terms: We're warning all patients with body piercing jewelry that this stuff can get in the way and, depending on what we do to you, may cause burns. If you won't take your jewelry off, then the second you're under anesthesia we'll take it off for you. If we do remove it for you we will try to replace it, but we invoke the unattended coat check rule, i.e., we are not responsible for any lost or stolen jewelry. Finally, if you wake up to find a team of physicians playing with your breast, don't sue us for sexual misconduct, they are only trying to get your nipple ring back in.

Huge Problems

Next to smoking, obesity is probably the BIGGEST cause of health problems in this country. Being IMMENSELY overweight increases potential health complications by a COLOSSAL percentage. Heavy people face ENORMOUS obstacles from societal discrimination, and I for one will try to avoid the temptation to make them the LARGE BUTT of any of my jokes.

However, I will relay some amazing stories of the difficulties faced by women who have clearly outgrown Lane Bryant.

Some women have little concept of their incredible girth. For every 250-pound woman with a sense of humor sporting an "I beat anorexia" button, there is a 300-pound woman who is deadly serious when she wears her "I'm not fat, I'm pregnant" button. When you start at 300 pounds and get pregnant, you wouldn't think that your body image would suffer greatly. But there she was, seven months pregnant and having some complications. Our now 340-pound heroine was in a communal examining room with only a curtain separating her from her neighbor. When she got up to go to the bathroom, the sight of her shocked the woman on the other side of the curtain. Discretion never came into play as the taken-aback neighbor observed out loud, "Woman, you are HUGE!" The 340-pounder cupped her stomach and gave her neighbor a profile view and defended herself. "Well, I am having twins."

When pregnant women get on the scale at the doctor's office, it isn't just so they can get upset at how much they weigh. There are medical benefits to tracking weight gain.

Sometimes it's necessary to know a woman's weight in order to prescribe the proper dosage of medicine. Finding out the exact weight can be a problem if the woman weighs more than the scale will register. There have been several cases of women who were so heavy that they had to be sent to the loading dock at the hospital to be weighed on the freight scale. I guess you know you're overweight when you can no longer be shipped by UPS.

Being weighed at the loading dock would be embarrassing enough. (Do you slip off your shoes before getting on the freight scale?) Even worse is when a woman is too big to fit into the CAT scan. A 500-pound woman with an ovarian cyst was in exactly this predicament. Fortunately for her, there are larger CAT scans than the ones at the hospital. Unfortunately for her, they are at the zoo. Zoos have a lot of money invested in their animals, and to protect their investments they will purchase expensive, oversized medical equipment. The zoo uses a giant CAT scan for the larger mammals: your elephants, hippos, 500-pound women. To add to this poor lady's misery, she had to buy a ticket to get in.

It's hard to imagine how some women get so big, considering they all swear that they don't eat that much. One might suspect they are lying. Certainly the doctor who went to do an abdominal check on a 400-pound woman and found a roast beef sandwich hidden under a layer of fat would suspect that the woman was lying. For some women chocolate goes right to their thighs; for this woman sandwiches go right to her stomach. They don't bother going inside the stomach, they just attach themselves to it.

The complications from obesity are potentially life-threatening. Even for the doctor. One dangerously large woman named Lindsay was a regular at her local hospital. Her diabetes was so uncontrolled that she was a regular visitor, and the residents there knew her routine. They also hoped to avoid her and would pass her off to an unsuspecting intern if the chance arose. Fortuitously for some resident, Dr. Charlie was the uninitiated intern on that night. Lindsay had called to prepare the hospital for her arrival, and the resident told Dr. Charlie, "Go get Lindsay's wheelbarrow." He may have thought he heard "wheelchair," but no, it was in fact "wheelbarrow," as Lindsay weighed a solid 600 pounds.

With plenty of help, Dr. Charlie was able to get Lindsay up to her personal, extra-large hospital bed, which was really a couple of beds put together. The last maneuver was to get Lindsay from the wheelbarrow onto the bed. Lindsay wasn't able to walk, but once standing, she could take one step. That was how she usually got into the bed. She would take one step and fall backwards onto the bed. No one told this to Dr. Charlie. His misfortune was to be posterially positioned as he helped her out of the wheelbarrow. She took her step and fell backwards onto the mattress. It must have felt a bit lumpy, as Dr. Charlie was between Lindsay and the mattress. He was flailing his arms and legs as he tried to get a breath. The other assistants quickly got Lindsay off him. Dr. Charlie was flat. Like a cartoon character who has been run over by a steamroller, the doctor was peeled off the bed and after a few seconds re-inflated to three dimensions ready to have a large combination safe fall out of a window on him.

It's not only in the physical sense that the pregnant, obese patient can put an obstetrician in an unusual position. If anyone should know how women get pregnant, it should be an obstetrician. But when the woman in question is so large that it would be physically . . . I mean the positions are limited to . . . who could reach? If you can explain it, you're doing better than most doctors. My wife had a theory: She thought they got a dining room table with extensions, and the woman got up on the table, and then the man removed a couple of leaves and he would stand in the middle section where the leaves used to be. A plausible suggestion. What I want to know is, where is that creativity when it comes to our sex life?

One nearly 700-pound pregnant patient was finally asked the ultimate question. She couldn't lay down flat because she had difficulty breathing. She couldn't get on top or the guy would have difficulty breathing. Her boyfriend had to bring two friends. She sat on the edge of the bed, and each friend grabbed a leg and held them apart. There. You had to ask, didn't you.

Generally, doctors will maintain the dignity of the patient no matter how heavy she might be. That may require extreme measures. As one gynecologist had the speculum in for an exam of a very overweight woman, he started singing to himself the great song from the movie *Spinal Tap*, "Big Bottom." If you are not familiar with it, the chorus goes something like:

Big Bottom/ She's Got 'em/ Talk about mud flaps my gal's got 'em.

It's a funny song even when you're not buried in a big bottom. The doctor could not get this song out of his head, and he began laughing. He started to get in one of those jags where you can't stop laughing and had to leave the room without saying anything, the woman stuck there, spread-eagle with a speculum inside of her.

The Bowels

It's a busy, chaotic hospital. People are running around yelling "STAT!" like they've got nothing better to do. Commotion reigns and yet, somehow, your doctor is able to get around with minimal effort. While a non-employee might need ten minutes to maneuver through all the traffic just to get a few yards to the Coke machine, hospital staff seem to appear an instant after they are summoned. On the one hand, it's a comfort to know that medical help can get to you quickly if needed. On the other hand, it's really kind of spooky. It's like having David Copperfield as your doctor.

Like all doctors, Karen has this mysterious ability. It's a power that is only effective at the hospital. She kind of just appears whenever I meet her there. I was curious about this and, one day, I followed her on her rounds and discovered the secret behind this power. The hospital has all these secret passages and unseen walkways that only those who work there know about. While we're waiting 15 minutes for an elevator to the second floor because we couldn't find the stairs, Karen and her cohorts are casually strolling up the secret staircase that only the locals know about.

I've concluded that hospitals are like Disneyland. On the surface it's all neat and clean, even sterile. The doctors are all knowledgeable and comforting. Things are done with ease and precision. But hidden away in the bowels are scurrying Mickey mice, trying to put on their surgical masks while sucking a last puff of their Camel. They're swearing about the customers, the lousy hours and the low pay. Every few seconds they have to dodge a golf cart carrying props for the surgery over in Operation Land. And we don't see any of it.

In fact, the similarities are so compelling, I suspect it won't be long before someone at Disney realizes the synergies. Disney will start taking over hospitals. Hospitals will be happy places. And, if you get the three-day pass, the hospital will only cost a little bit more than it does now.

Of Penises And Prostates

Years of study and training on the female anatomy; pushing uteruses, feeling cervixes and the like, have made Karen uniquely qualified when it comes to handling a penis. "Huh?" you ask. Well, I don't understand it either, but one of the duties of an OB is to perform circumcisions on the boys they deliver. Why this isn't a job for a surgeon or the pediatrician, I don't know. It's like there was a big meeting to decide who would do this procedure and the OBs lost.

OBS: Let the surgeons do it.

SURG: (Derisively) That's not surgery. It's trimming. Have the peds do it.

PEDS: We do shots. I don't think we even own a pair of scissors. The OBs are always cutting the cord. They know about cutting.

OBS: We're so bad at it we give the job to the dads. We deal with women. We haven't seen a penis since med school.

SURG: Don't give me your personal problems. We're busy handling emergencies. We can't be bothered with this. To paraphrase Scotty on *Star Trek*, I'm a doctor not a barber.

PEDS: I guess we could do them. It's just that we have minimal malpractice and . . . Oops! Spilled the coffee again, I'm sorry, I'm just a little jittery . . .

OBS: FINE! We'll do them.

So the OBs are responsible for circumcisions whether they

are medically knowledgeable about the area or not. One female OB clearly wasn't. She watched in shock after cutting off the foreskin as the outer folds of skin collapsed in a pile at the base of the penis. She held up the penis and pulled up the skin, but it fell down again as if it were a loose sock. She tried one more time, hoping perhaps that on the third try some tape would magically grow out of the penis to hold the skin on. When it didn't, she called the urologist, who told her not to worry, it would correct itself.

Another OB was not aware that a baby penis can be too small to be circumcised. She carried out the procedure as the mother stood by. A miscalculation, and she ended up cutting the penis itself. Afraid that she had caused irreparable harm, she told the mother that she was going to quickly call a urologist. The mother remained calm. "Don't worry about it," she said. "It wasn't going to grow that much. You should see the father."

Probably the main reason the OB has ended up being responsible is that the OB, at least in the case of first babies, has established a comfort level with the patients that the pediatrician doesn't yet have. Although it is a rather routine procedure, it can be a very emotional one for the parents. Overwhelmed with their new parental responsibility, they face a decision that they probably hadn't considered: Do they want a circumcision? Don't they? Does it hurt? Will the boy be scarred? Physically? Emotionally? Will he automatically be Jewish if you do this?

There is little to be concerned about. Surely it does hurt, but if you ask any man if he was traumatized by his own circumcision, I doubt he'll be able to give you any details of the event. Nowadays, a topical anesthetic is used to reduce the pain. And no, it doesn't make a child Jewish, it just makes him look Jewish.

The biggest concern regarding circumcision is doing one that isn't wanted. In some hospitals where there are a lot of births, a group of newborns will be routinely lined up on special circ boards so that the day's snipping can all be done at once. A fore disassembly line. Unfortunately, there are times when a child is altered against the parent's wishes. There is no gluing it back on. The hospital will try to come up with some excuse to explain why the circ was done. Any of the following have been approaches that were used to reassure angry parents:

- "Did you notice how tight the foreskin was? Oh, yes. The rest of the penis was getting pinched. The doctors felt the foreskin had to come off. It's not uncommon."
- "The larger ones need breathing room. Were you circumcised yourself, sir? . . . Yes? Oh my. Like father like son."
- or: "The larger ones need breathing room. Were you circumcised yourself, sir? . . . *No?* Oh my. Well, sometimes, if it's really going to get large they keep the foreskin on to keep it from becoming too unwieldy."
- "On some kids it just falls off."
- "We all felt it was such an attractive penis it would be a shame to cover it up."
- "Teenagers do such crazy things—there's body piercing and cults or even just drinking too much and accepting a dare—so let's just say we saved you and your son a future argument."

The one advantage for the OBs in doing the circumcisions is that they won't ever be confronted by the results of their work. There aren't many men coming to see the gynecologist. Just those that want to be women. Men undergoing a sex change will go to the gynecologist for estrogen shots as they go through the process of becoming a woman. It might be a little discombobulating to women in the waiting room when the person next to them is a man, and the assistant calls, "Joe, come on back. The doctor will see you now."

Then there are the ex-men. Not the comic book characters. The former men who have become women. I'll bet you never thought about where a former man goes for her annual physical. Well, neither did this one female gynecologist until a sex-change patient showed up on her exam table. Things were more confusing for Dr. Linda because the office staff had neglected to mention that Erica used to be Eric.

The doctor began by getting a patient history from the attractive woman.

"Have you had annual Pap smears?" asked the doctor.

"No, I've never had a Pap smear before."

The doctor thought this unusual for a woman in her 40s.

"No children?" continued the doctor.

"One child."

"One child? Then certainly you had a Pap smear."

"No."

"Maybe you just don't remember." suggested the doctor searching for some explanation.

"No. Today will be my first one. I used to be a man. I had a child as a man."

Doctor Linda was in mild shock. She had never encountered this before and, as some people will do when they get flustered, she just started talking.

"Ooooohh! Of course. Now I see. Of course you didn't have a Pap smear—Why would you? Ha! That's pretty funny. Because you're a man, right! I don't know what I was thinking. I'm so used to having women who were women all the time. How boring is that? Huh? It's a rut. Day after day, women, women, women. But you? You're a man. WERE a man. Obviously now . . . not. Who could tell? . . . Would you excuse me for a minute . . . Pap smear. Ha! . . . "

The doctor stepped out and shut the door behind her in mid-ramble. Then after catching her breath she began dressing down the office manager. She yelled in a whisper through clenched teeth, kind of how your Mom used to yell at you in the grocery store.

"How come nobody told me that's a MAN!?"

The office manager was stunned. She apologized, but there was nothing to be done. Dr. Linda thought about switching with one of her male partners, but then realized she should just be a professional and do a regular exam. The doctor did a Pap smear and suggested Erica go somewhere else for a prostate exam. She was impressed by the plastic surgeon's work and complimented Erica on how realistic it looked. Very pleased with how things went, Erica became a regular patient and one of Dr. Linda's favorites. Erica has sent friends of like circumstance, and Dr. Linda has built up a reputation in the sex-change community. In fact, she has considered advertising herself as "Dr. L. OB/GYN: A doctor for women and the men who want to be one."

Lawsuits

The thing that bothers doctors about lawsuits isn't that they can be held responsible for their mistakes, it's that they may be held responsible for something they had no control over. I would not be surprised if an OB has been sued for the "pain and suffering of labor and childbirth." Or perhaps a damages case for "recklessly bringing a child into the world for which the mother had no capacity to be responsible."

Aside from being blamed for the blameless, doctors fret over lawsuits being brought for ridiculously petty things. These don't often result in large judgments, but they take up precious hours that should be devoted to the practice of medicine. One example: A woman came into the office for her postpartum checkup. Her doctor realized that a staple from her C-section had been left in her. He pointed it out—the patient was unaware of it—and excused himself to go and get a staple remover. (Official, technical term—Stapleoscopizer) When he returned, the woman was dressed and headed out the door. The doctor asked where she was going. He needed to remove the staple. She said, "No way. That's my evidence." She no doubt headed straight to her lawyer to strategize on the large sum they could extract for all her imaginary pain and suffering. It would probably get dismissed as a frivolous lawsuit, but that doctor would either have to spend time in court or in negotiations over a settlement. And tense negotiations those would be:

LAWYER: Aside from the physical pain of having a staple shot into her, my client suffered mental anguish, emotional scarring, and we expect a sum of $500,000.00.

DOCTOR AND HIS INSURANCE COMPANY: First of all, she was under anesthesia when the staple was put in, and we feel that her mental anguish and emotional scarring are worth $8.53.

LAWYER: You insult us. Look at this woman. She'll have to use paper clips the rest of her life because of the stress whenever she looks at a staple. Twelve bucks.

DOC AND INSURERS: Done.

I think there would be a lot fewer lawsuits if patients realized that when they sue their doctor they are—follow closely—suing their doctor. You probably realize that, but there are plenty of people who think that the doctor himself isn't affected by a lawsuit. They must think that some invisible monolith is getting the lawsuit because there are patients who will show up for treatment after bringing a suit against a doctor and act like nothing ever happened. When the doctor refuses to see them, they get insulted. More than one doctor has told me stories of women wondering why they weren't being seen. One woman, adamant that she be seen, told the doctor that the lawsuit "has nothing to do with you." It just had something to do with the way he practiced medicine. Another woman, when queried as to why she was coming to see a doctor she had recently sued justified it with, "I'm not suing you. My lawyer's suing you." That's kind of like the doctor giving the patient a shot and telling her, "I'm not hurting you, it's that darn pointy needle."

As expected, doctors were a bit touchy when I asked about the subject of malpractice. They didn't think there was anything funny about it. However, when you break the word down; mal—from the latin meaning "bad," practice—from the English meaning "practice," you realize that it doesn't have to be a tragic outcome or horrible doctor error. Malpractice can be something smaller that didn't really affect anyone's health. Like that missed staple. Don't call it malpractice, call it mistakes you got away with. Doctors were willing to confess to a few of those. Here they are.

Here Comes Another One

Dr. R. was very happy with how the delivery went.
After a relatively short labor the mother pushed out a baby
girl. The baby was a bit small at six pounds, one ounce, but
that was nothing to worry about. While they were doing all
the routine tests on the baby, Dr. R. tried to get the mother to
push out the placenta, but it wasn't coming so easily. She
reached inside the Mom to see what might be the holdup.
After a few seconds of feeling around, Dr. R. gave a scared
yelp and quickly yanked her hand out.

It's generally not a good sign when your doctor screams in
surprise. And once a doctor has screamed, there is no legitimate coverup. Sure, the doctor might say, "I just sat on a cold
stethoscope" or "That wasn't me. It was the sphygmo-
manometer squealing." But that won't fool anyone. Dr. R. was
stuck having to tell the truth.

"What's the matter?" asked the patient.

"A hand grabbed me." said Dr. R.

"WHAT?" yelled everyone in the room.

Dr. R. explained, "I don't know how we missed it, but it
looks like you're having twins."

As rare as it may be to miss the occurrence of twins, it is
almost unheard of, when expecting twins, to find only one
baby. That's what happened, however, to a doctor who we will
call Dr. Stan. He was doing a scheduled Cesarean to deliver
twins. With the husband at his side, Dr. Stan opened up the
mother, and it immediately became obvious that the doctor
had overestimated the number of babies Mom was carrying.

What had likely occurred was a misreading of an early ultrasound. As the sole passenger was removed from the uterus, the shocked father asked, "What happened to our other baby?"

Silence.

Then after a second, a quick-thinking Dr. Stan calmly replied, "It's not unheard of for one baby to consume the other one."

Didn't We Learn That In Med School

Being an intern is not fun. Internship is when you're supposed to get five years of medical experience in one calendar year. Although that sounds impossible, training programs have discovered that, when they don't sleep at night, interns can triple their workload. You're a little groggy in the delivery room sometimes, so what? You get used to it. Or as happened to one intern, you fall asleep on a woman's thigh while sewing an episiotomy. The woman was very nice. She told the nurse not to wake him, "He's had a hard night."

Most of the time the doctor can push through it. Don't get sick, though. That will exacerbate the exhaustion, and then you could start making mistakes. That was the problem for Dr. N. as she staggered into her fifth delivery of the night. Four boys had come into the world by her hands since midnight. It was now 6 a.m. She had a fever and was bleary-eyed and knew she shouldn't be there, but residency is supposed to be hard, so Dr. N was going to stick it out. Thankfully, it was an easy delivery. Everything went smoothly and quickly, and as the baby popped out, Dr. N. caught it, held it up, and as a matter of rote said, "It's a boy." She then handed the baby to the nurse for cleaning and dressing, and she excused herself to go to the call room and collapse.

The husband and wife didn't notice the doctor's hasty departure. They were too excited about having a boy. They had four girls at home and were thrilled with their first boy. The Dad had already made some calls and was headed to the lobby to make some more when the nurses went to give some standard tests to the newborn. Suddenly there was a flurry of activity and the doctor was paged to return to the delivery room STAT.

When she got there, the doctor confirmed the nurse's diagnosis. She gave the family the bad news.

"We went to do some tests and realized the baby is a girl."

"A girl?" asked the incredulous parents.

"Yes."

"And you had to do some tests before you realized this?"

"Well, no. Just in the process of doing the tests, the baby was undressed and the nurses realized it then."

The nurses had called the doctor back in because they didn't want to be the ones to break it to the parents. The parents were very gracious about it and glad that their misconception didn't go on longer. They were lucky to have discovered it then. Otherwise they may not have known until around age six, when they would question their "son"'s fascination with hair clips and nail polish.

How To Remove A Uterus

The surgery was going well. The woman was in for a vaginal hysterectomy, or "vag-hyst" in the lexicon of doctors in a hurry who don't have the time to say all the syllables. A vag-hyst is more time-consuming, yet less invasive than a standard hysterectomy. Instead of cutting the woman open to take out the uterus, it is removed through the vagina. This probably has all kinds of significance for healing, and insurance. For our concern, it affects the position in which the surgeon performs the operation.

When a doctor does a regular hysterectomy, they have to stand over the patient to do the work. When they do a vag-hyst, they can either stand or sit or alternate between the two, depending on how their back is feeling and how much leverage they need. In this case, the doctor began in the sitting position, but had pushed away the stool and had been standing for a while. There was only one segment of the uterus that was still attached. The other points where it had been cut were being held by clamps. In an effort to get better leverage, the surgeon decided to sit down.

There is no specific training for the job of stool nurse. Maybe it's covered in one class very early in nursing school. Basically, what you need to know is that if the stool is not right behind the doctor when she goes to sit down, one should quickly be put under her. Here, a nurse tried. She underestimated the strength of her leg, however, and when she kicked the stool it rolled under the doctor's descending butt and right on past before contact was ever made. The doctor—assuming the stool had stopped underneath her—continued to move into the sitting position. She stopped only when her butt landed on the floor. Since she had been holding onto the clamps as she went to sit, the force of her backwards fall was enough to pull the woman's uterus out. There the doctor lay, sprawled on the O.R. floor with the patient's uterus on top of her. Another successful surgery as performed by a graduate of Clown Medical College.

Now Where Was I?

One doctor I interviewed for this book was more forthcoming than most doctors about his mistakes. He told me about the time he fell asleep while taking a woman's medical history. Those things tend to be rather boring, and after a night on call, it's perfectly understandable. He also confessed to the grave error of giving the good news-bad news prognosis to a patient in the wrong order. A pregnant woman was bleeding in her first trimester. The doctor found that the woman had in fact miscarried. He had also discovered it was twins. He told the mother that it was twins first. The mother got very excited. Then he had to give her doubly bad news. He won't do that again.

His most embarrassing *faux pas*, however, was when a nervous teenager got in the stirrups on her first visit to the gynecologist. He was about to examine her when an important phone call came in. The doctor excused himself to answer the call in his office. Two minutes later he hung up the phone and looked at the clock. Lunchtime! He went to the corner deli, had a sandwich, read the paper and sauntered back for his afternoon appointments. Upon his return he asked his assistant for his schedule. She suggested that he should probably finish with his morning patients first. He ran back to the room and there was the teenager, still up in the stirrups. Being her first time, she just assumed this was normal procedure.

And Now
Without Looking

There are people who can do many things at once. I
myself am a Type A personality. I read while I ride the stationary bike, make phone calls while cleaning the kitchen,
fairly typical Type A stuff. Realistically, I'm probably only an
A-. If I were a true Type A, I would probably be trying to
clean the kitchen while I rode the stationary bike. I suspect
that a high percentage of doctors are Type A's. They have so
much to do under so much time pressure that it seems it
would take a Type A just to make it through med school. Then
in a hospital, things only get worse. An OB has to be aware of
many things going on at once and has to be able to deal with
them all simultaneously. Sometimes they can't.

One overwhelmed OB was trying to induce a patient who
had a history of medical problems. The patient was hooked up
to a fetal monitor, and her IVs were in and dripping. The monitor was the external kind, but monitoring was very difficult,
as the patient was a very large woman. Her family was all
there, and they were chatting up the doctor while he attempt-
ed to feel uterine response to his palpitating of the fundus.
(The fundus is part of the uterus. The word is derived from
sarcastic, laboring women who often say, "Some fun-dis is.")
To clarify this picture: he was standing next to the bed,
kneading the woman's belly while looking the other direction
at a monitor and trying to talk to the family at the same time.
It's not surprising, then, that when the patient sheepishly
mumbled something to the doctor, he couldn't respond with
any more than a "What?" while he kept focused on the moni-

tor. A similar exchange took place again, and after the second "What?" the patient exclaimed in a loud voice, "Dr. . . . that's my breast!" A quick-thinking doctor might have said, "Yes, I know, and it keeps getting in the way of the fundus!" Instead, he just turned red, apologized and prepared himself for a lifetime of anatomy books as Christmas presents from his coworkers.

A   W E E K E N D   A T   H O M E

How to be a Doctor in Your Spare Time

Mixing Business And Pleasure

Carol Leifer, a comedienne who is perhaps best known as the inspiration for the character of Elaine on *Seinfeld*, has a great joke about what she imagines life would be like married to a male gynecologist. She suspects it would be difficult to ignite his amorous flames. His wife could greet him at the door in some sexy lingerie, love clearly on her mind, and he would dismiss her with, "Honey, if I so much as *look* at another vagina . . . ."

It sure points out the downside to a job most men think has some illicit benefits. At some point, any job can become mundane no matter the matter at hand. Personally, I can't believe a baseball player would ever want a day off, but they do. So it wasn't surprising, then, when I heard about the two OB/GYNs who went to a strip joint and hung out in the back while the rest of the bachelor party ogled the women from the front row. It wasn't anything they didn't see too many times a day.

In this case, it perturbed the dancers. They were strippers. They wanted respect. They asked the guys in the front row what the problem with the other two was. Were they gay? When told they were gynecologists, the women all made a beeline to them to ask questions and get advice. There they were, two lonely gynecologists, getting the kind of attention most men would get in that place only with a bulge in their pants that came from a wad of twenties. They had to leave before the rest of the customers complained. And before the grateful women started stuffing bills in their boxers.

Not all male OB/GYNs are so jaded as to ignore strippers or

171

other sexual icons when they encounter them. They can become just as flustered as the rest of us. Case in point—a gynecologist who found himself sitting next to a familiar-looking woman in a first-class seat on an airplane. There was the usual chitchat about the weather and where you're from, and the whole time the doctor was trying to place her. It was driving him crazy, and just as he was about to ask, it hit him. It was Marilyn Chambers. Yes, that Marilyn Chambers. The porno film star. The doctor didn't know what to say. He became very red as he tried a compliment. "I like your movies." Then, realizing he was sounding a bit lecherous, added, " . . . professionally. You got me interested in gynecology." It would have been better to have been lecherous. It was a long, uncomfortable flight.

Pity the poor single male gynecologist who can't hide from his profession in the dating world. Our pal Todd had spotted the love of his life across the room at one of those drug rep functions. With enough liquid fortification, he meandered over to the comely lass and struck up a conversation. It seemed to be going well, at least until she found out what Todd did. Then she couldn't help but use the opportunity to tell him a bit about her dysplasia. It seemed innocent enough but upon hearing that, Todd beat a quick retreat. The woman must not have understood that dysplasia is caused by a sexually transmitted virus. Not the kind of information you want to give out over your first drink. Or maybe you do. It could have been a subtle yet effective way to get rid of a doctor who was hitting on her.

It's not just with women that business intrudes on pleasure. Men have a voyeuristic fascination with what a gynecologist does. None of us is far removed emotionally from our teenage years. It's one of the dream jobs for a teenage boy, ranking right behind rock star and professional athlete. They are thinking, "Women, getting naked in your office all day . . . Cool!" Just the thought turns even the most respectable teenager into Beavis or Butthead. That was discovered by an OB friend named Evan who, in an effort to remain youthful, attends a weeklong guitar camp every summer. His first summer, he stayed in the dorms with mostly teenage boys. At first eyed with suspicion, Evan became the most popular guy in camp once the boys found out what he did for a living. He was the Pied Guitarist. Boys followed him all over camp. Then, at night, he would hold court in his cabin. Sitting Buddha-like, the wise elder would impart his wisdom about the mysterious, even mythical, vagina.

Enjoying the attention, Evan embellished and glamorized his profession for the kids' benefit. He would say things like: "I only take women patients who are at least as hot as Pamela Anderson"; "The biggest problem women come to the office for is that they need a doctor to help them find their clitoris"; or "To do a proper breast exam you need to use your tongue." After a day of this, though, Evan got a little tired of the attention and he had to burst the kids' bubble. "Most of my practice is made up of 80-year-olds or overweight women who are so big they have trouble finding anything below their belt. And if you use your tongue for a breast exam, you've got some explaining to do if you want to keep your license." Then he went on to give a little dissertation on vaginal discharge and the intricacies of secondary insurance. By dinner, the boys had stopped talking clap in favor of Clapton. On subsequent trips to guitar camp, Evan said he was an accountant.

Gynecologists do find that there are times when they must lie about their true profession in anticipation of public reaction. Such was the case with one practitioner on a family vacation in New England. The family visited a chocolate factory. At the end of the tour, the tour guide would always ask one visitor from the group to tell his or her profession, and then a chocolatier (or whatever you call them) would whip up a confection in a shape honoring that profession. The tour guide pointed to our friendly gynecologist and asked, "Sir, what do you do?" He wisely deferred to a commodity trader, which allowed the cocoa engineer to make a cute little chocolate pork belly. It doesn't sound very appetizing, but it was a whole lot better than what could have been. Although, I imagine a box of chocolate vaginas could be a big seller. Certainly, it would be cause for Forrest Gump to alter his life-affirming philosophy.

Lovely Parting Gifts

When everything goes smoothly, a birth can be a thing of beauty. Everyone in the delivery room is filled with emotion and wonder. While it is a divine work, the doctor who has presided over this miraculous event deserves some of the gratitude that is bestowed upon her by the appreciative parents. She also deserves a cookie. Well, maybe more than one cookie. Probably a whole tray of cookies. And that is what she often finds when she arrives home after a hard day at the office or hospital.

A tray of cookies and other sugary desserts is typical of the gifts Karen receives from patients following a delivery. Other popular items are: fruit baskets and wine, cheese and pasta baskets. Apparently, Karen's patients think she's hungry. Like I said, I haven't seen her work, but maybe she does something to give patients this impression. Maybe as she implores the patient to push, and catches the baby, she is wolfing down a sandwich.

If that's the case, it doesn't seem to bother the patients, who write highly complimentary notes to accompany the food they send. Actually, if the cards are to be believed, 90% of them are written by the infants themselves. A typical one might say:

"Thank you so much for delivering me into the world last September 13 at 2:30 in the morning. You were very reassuring to my Mom and Dad, Mary and Tom Smith. Your encouragement and compassion were instrumental in getting Mom

through the delivery. How serendipitous that you were on call that night. Love, Tom Jr."

For a three-week-old to use words like "serendipitous" is really quite amazing. Karen seems to deliver an inordinate number of prodigies. And it's not just the vocabulary. The handwriting is a beautiful cursive. Karen suspects that the mothers really write these notes, but I say that even if the babies are just dictating, it's still quite an impressive command of the language.

There is no standard protocol that requires a thank you gift for your doctor after a delivery. It's not like tipping your waiter. You don't have to give more for twins or an extra 10% for a C-section. Patients send these because they are generous and truly thankful for the care they received. And it does mean a lot to Karen. Large paychecks go only so far as compensation. A nice "thank you" means a lot. Often she gets more than that. The praise heaped on her is lavish. Cards have been sent calling her "sensational," "the consummate professional," "the best doctor in the country," "the greatest doctor ever." Karen's not one to boast, but who is to say that she isn't? There are no records kept that would prove otherwise. ACOG (The American College of Obstetrics and Gynecology) doesn't keep track of "Most successful deliveries—season" or "Total weight of babies—career." So you can't argue against my wife being the best. I guess the best way to determine the best doctor would be to find out who gets the most cookie trays and cheese platters sent to them. Instead of doing a lengthy survey, I offer this theorem from which Karen is exempted— the most appreciated doctors are the fattest. Keep that in mind when choosing your OB.

Want Ads

You should see the mail that awaits Karen's return home from work. It is through the mail that I have found that my wife is an object of desire. Not just by me, but by hundreds of other men. I'm not just bragging here. Karen is desired for her supple long fingers, the way she wields a knife, and mostly for a bod that won't quit even in scrubs.

I'm married to a gorgeous spy. And my name is Bond. James . . . .

Sorry. Went off into a little fantasy of my own there. Truth is, Karen is wanted by men because she is wanted by women. Her supple fingers and surgical skills aside, it's the female body that seems to bring in the women as patients. All the women doctors Karen knows are very busy, while many of the older, more established men have practices that are languishing. How can these men get business booming again? Hire a woman doctor, or become one.

The competition for female doctors is fierce. There are headhunters who try to entice doctors to move from their current practices to more lucrative ones. Nearly every week Karen gets a phone call or something in the mail about "Double your salary! Fantastic opportunity in an abandoned, quaint, western mining town." We have no intention of moving, though I can't help but entertain the offers. They are for ridiculous amounts of money. Moving to a suburb of a perfectly lovely city like Chicago could offer a 50% increase in Karen's income. That's tempting. For urban/suburban types like us, the location is at least an improvement on the ones

177

Karen got a few years ago. Those would be for:

- "OB/GYN opportunity in Farflungsville, Montana—$300,000/yr."

Or, • "Winter paradise in Alaska's spectacular interior glacial region. Triple your current salary. Eight weeks of vacation. Quiet evenings communing with native elk."

Karen would reject the offers out of hand. I enjoyed contemplating the possibilities. I had visions of counting our money under the northern lights. I would prod Karen, "Doesn't desolate tundra have a certain ennui, dear?" When that didn't coerce her, I'd bring out my big gun, "At parties, we'd never have to make a run for ice." My persuasion skills are a bit lacking.

Those kinds of offers don't come in much any more. I think they go to the men. Less in demand in the big cities as more women come into the field, the men are banished to our Siberias. Those without skirts are enticed to the outskirts.

I'm not sure how these little places like Farflungsville, Montana are getting the money they offer, anyway. I can only assume that the independent militias hiding there aren't putting all their money into munitions and canned goods. Communities that are seeking health care professionals should realize that money alone is not a strong enough lure. A stray gynecologist, alone in a rural setting, wouldn't feel safe no matter how much money they had. Gynecologists need to be around other gynecologists. The old saw—to get a gynecologist you need a gynecologist—is true even if it's not an old saw. My bit of advice is that they make it a saw, see. If you or someone you know is in a small community looking for a doctor, venture into the nearest big city with a blow dart or tranquilizer gun and capture yourself a doctor. Then that doctor and a bundle of cash can be used to entice another doctor into a contract. When the second doctor has signed, you can release the captive doctor back into his native habitat. I know it sounds extreme, but it's not as radical as health care reform.

Always Learning

The longer your OB has been in private practice— dealing with real-life patients and diverse situations, honing his skills and growing in experience and maturity—the more out of touch he is. Medicine is constantly changing, and the change comes from the researchers and the academics. An OB in private practice, many years removed from medical school, may be entrenched in his ways. He might be relying on outdated procedures, unaware that there has been a major breakthrough in the whole baby delivery system that has been in use for the past, oh, let's say . . . FOREVER!

Because of this, you'll be pleased to know, your doctor is required to keep up with advances in the field through CME— Continuing Medical Education. Every doctor is required to get a certain number of points of CME credit each year. Yes, they have a credit card with a magnetic strip and points are added to it for each class depending on how hard it is to stay awake for the lecture. If they don't get enough points in a year, they could get put on probation. Miss the requirement for two straight years, and their license could get suspended. Get pulled over a third time and you'll find yourself in the hoosegow with some big, ugly obstetricians who are doing hard time.

Fortunately, for Karen and her colleagues, there are all kinds of ways to earn CME credits. There are weekly lectures at the hospital, drug-company sponsored dinners, hospital staff breakfasts. You get credit for watching *E.R.* so you can see they aren't that strict. Just don't try claiming credit for a repeat episode. The AMA isn't stupid.

The main method for getting CME credits, however, is the conference. This is where doctors get together for three or four days and have thrilling lectures like "Congenital Uterovaginal Anomalies and You." Sounds boring, right? Only because I didn't present it the way it's presented in the brochures—"Come learn about Congenital Uterovaginal Anomalies in SUNNY JAMAICA!" It's all in how you sell it.

There are two basic types of conferences—serious and crib. The serious conference has courses that tackle advanced surgical skills or unique issues and procedures that a general practitioner wouldn't otherwise have an opportunity to learn about. You can tell it's a serious conference if you spot lectures about things you've never heard of, like, "Enterocele Repair." It's serious if there are classes about things a hypochondriac would never admit to having, like "Abdominal Sacrocolpopexy for Vaginal Vault Prolapse." It's serious if there are courses like "Hysteroscopic-Resectoscopic Resection of Myoma, Uterine Synechia, Septate Uterus, and Endometrial Ablation" which you can only take if you've passed the prerequisite, "How to pronounce Hysteroscopic-Resectoscopic Resection of Myoma, Uterine Synechia, Septate Uterus, and Endometrial Ablation," class. It's serious if there is a lecture on parts of the anatomy that you didn't realize have their own name, like "Management of the Anterior Vaginal Segment." I'm not certain, but I think an injury to the anterior vaginal segment is what ended Joe Montana's career.

On the other hand, a crib conference will offer very generic topics and classes that even a lay person could participate in. Topics like "When Mr. Sperm Meets Mrs. Egg" or "Taking a Pulse: How Slow is Too Slow?" are topics for a crib conference. Other classes at a crib conference clearly state, "This is your vacation." Classes of this nature are: "Delivering Babies by an Ocean—Is It Different?," "The Effects of Tanning on Pre-Menopausal Women" and "Understanding the Patient with a Jamaican Accent."

Most doctors have a practice that gives them an allowance and time off to spend attending at least one conference a year. There is no paucity of both types of conferences from which to choose. Each day a new brochure arrives in the mail. Some entice you with exotic locales in the Caribbean or on a cruise through Alaska, while others entice doctors with the faculty that will be giving the course.

Karen likes to go for the good courses. Some of these conference lecturers are like rock stars to other doctors. Karen will read the list of faculty at some of the conferences and start to salivate.

"Oooh, Dr. Von Nottingham will be there. He wrote the book on urinary incontinence!"

To which I could only reply, "Yeah, well, I'm not surprised there's only one book. Urinary incontinence just doesn't inspire many authors." Strangely, it has been the impetus for some great vacations.

Play That Funky Music

The beeper was at one time an instrument of prestige. Doctors were the only ones who used them. If you wore one, you were instantly granted the respect that four years of medical school affords you. Then, drug dealers started carrying beepers. Suddenly anyone with a beeper was either a highly respected member of society or a criminal. It was up to the observer to figure out which one you were. There was no distinguishing symbol for the observer. No "left hip is a doctor, right hip a drug runner" to help you tell one from the other. Fortunately, no one has ever approached Karen and tried to buy some crack.

Eventually the beeper became required attire for all professions and lost both its prestige and stigma. Thanks to their ubiquity, new features were added. People at the orchestra didn't want to be disturbed by a series of beeps every time the painter one seat over had a client decide to change the color of their foyer. So the vibrate mode was invented.

Vibrate mode is the little reward for having to work. Positioned properly, and with enough calls, the vibrating pager can be a surprising yet fun way to tone up your muscles and stimulate those hard-to-reach areas. A little joy buzzer for the hips and thighs. Forget Jane Fonda or any other workout video you may subscribe to. A forgotten vibrating beeper in the pants is a sure way to get you moving. And no longer are you disturbed by that annoying beep at a concert. Instead you get a side show by watching your neighbor suddenly jump out of his seat.

Out of necessity, the choice of beeps has become varied too. With the potential for, say, 27 beepers in one room, it was imperative to come up with different beeps so that each time someone's pager went off, all 27 people were not alarmed. So now beepers can be programmed to play all kinds of sounds. Karen can request a different beep for a different patient need. I think she could even program songs in. For example, she could have it play "Happy Birthday" for a woman in labor, while it would play "I Want to Hold Your Hand" for a woman who won't be doing anything more than that unless she can get a new birth control prescription fast. In fact there are so many possibilities with the marvelous little pager that I can readily envision a day when instead of disturbing a concert, the pager will *be* the concert. Symphony for pager in D minor No. 7, "The OB/GYN Symphony," Karen Jaffe conducting. Are you ready to rock and roll . . . I mean vibrate?

Turning Off The Beeper

Karen has a little tradition which I imagine other doctors mimic in some manner. When vacation comes, she heralds it with a tug on her beeper that yanks it off her belt. She then raises the pesky annoyance high in the air and with a flick of the thumb, turns it off and declares, "Vacation has begun!" Her joy is tempered only by the fact that she will have missing wallet syndrome (MWS) all vacation. Vacation is the most common time to have MWS. It is usually brought on by feeling the pocket where you normally keep your wallet and realizing it's not there. Your heart sinks as your mind races to the calls you have to place to the credit card companies and the spousal lecture you'll have to endure. You break out in a cold sweat, experience chills and wild mood swings and then, after an agonizing half a second, you remember that you sensibly left it in the hotel room safe while you were scuba diving. The syndrome subsides. That is how most doctors feel without their beeper.

A responsible physician will be certain that he is on vacation, or at least not on call, when he turns off his beeper. If they aren't, they might end up like Dr. C., who, after a long day at the hospital, needed to get some rest. He thought it was a partner's night on call, so he turned off his beeper and, just to make sure he wasn't disturbed, unplugged his phone and went to sleep.

He was startled awake by a loud pounding at his front door. He jumped out of bed and glanced out his window to see who was raising such a ruckus. The first thing he noticed was the flashing police lights. Then he heard the police megaphone. "Dr. C. You are on call! Please come out." What they should have said is "Come out with your hands up after scrubbing for surgery."

Being accessible is an important part of being on call. It's not enough that you get the page, you must be able to answer it too. That aspect of the beeper was lost one sunny Saturday afternoon by an OB who had some work to do around the house.

Dr. W. lived in South Carolina, right along the inland waterway. Although he had yet to purchase a boat, he did have a dock. Part of his dock was of the floating variety. As opposed to a permanent structure, a floating dock is designed to rise and sink in conjunction with the extreme tides. Dr. W. had to do some work on his using some electric tools. He had no power source at his dock, but his neighbor had an outlet right off his pier only a few yards away, so he decided to move his dock over and hitch it to the neighboring pier. The good doctor was not concerned about being paged. If his beeper went off, he could simply walk the few yards back to his home and make the call.

The only problem seemed a minor one. How would he get his wharf to the neighbor's? A quick calculation, and Dr. W. accurately figured that in the calm waters, it would only take a couple of paddles and he would be there. All worked as planned, and the doctor had a productive afternoon of float repair. He was just unhitching his dock for the quick trip back when his pager sounded, alerting him to a woman in labor. With the waters now at high tide and moving quickly, our hero assumed it would only be a few seconds for him to ride back and reattach to his pier.

The second he let the rope go he knew he had miscalculated. His permanent dock didn't jut out as far as his neighbor's, and the current was stronger than anticipated, at what was now high tide. Dr. W. made a valiant attempt to grab onto his pier, but just missed it. His float started picking up speed as the current carried him toward the center of the waterway.

His wife was watching this whole thing happen and immediately jumped to action. She paged her husband. He's on a runaway float, there's a woman in labor, and his wife is paging him to . . . what? Remind him to pick up a gallon of milk on his way downstream?

To give her the benefit of the doubt, perhaps she was hoping he had it all under control and was just going for a little joy ride, and even had the portable phone with him. But she was paging him to their home number! Even if he had the portable phone, he couldn't call himself. Clearly she wasn't thinking clearly. Her next move was much better. She jumped in the car and drove downstream to some neighbors'.

The doctor was, by now, a mile along the raging river. He was trying to get the attention of someone along the shore. As luck would have it, someone was having a party on their verandah. He signaled for help. They smiled and waved back, happy to acknowledge the friendly rafter.

By this time Mrs. W. had gotten another neighbor to get his boat and some rope and chase after her husband. The boat was able to catch up to him, and Dr. W. tied the rope around the floating dock. However, it was a big dock, about 25 by 25 feet, and the boat had a small engine. Now there was a dock and a boat sailing downstream.

And the beeper keeps going off. The answering service paging again. Another woman in labor. Mrs. W. racing ahead, looking for a spot to grab them. And finally, another boat to the rescue. This one larger and with a lot of horsepower. It was all needed. The current was so strong, it took over an hour to pull back upstream what took only ten minutes to go downstream. Doctor W. made it to the hospital in time for the delivery.

The next day he ran into the head nurse at the hospital. "I was at a party yesterday and I thought I saw you floating by.

I said to my friend, 'I think that's the doc on the dock.'"

It was only the first of many doc dock jokes that would be told at his expense.

A Few More Calls

If you aren't able to turn the beeper off, you are bound to get a few more calls when you get home. Although these may not have come in the middle of the night they left the doctor as confused, as if she had just been awakened from a deep sleep. Again I will take over and give the response I would have liked, had I been the doctor.

PATIENT: I'm four months pregnant and my stomach was bothering me, so I took some Pepto Bismol. Is that OK?
DOCTOR MARC: Oh . . . My . . . God! You say you already took it? If only you'd called before. Now your baby will be pink.

PATIENT: What's the cure for breast cancer?
DOCTOR MARC: Do you have breast cancer?
PATIENT: No. I'm just sitting around with some friends, and we were wondering what the cure is.
DOCTOR MARC: The cure is to quit sitting around. Go do something.

PATIENT: I keep trying to pee, but nothing's coming out.
DOCTOR MARC: Maybe you don't really have to go.
PATIENT: Oh. O.K. Thanks.
DOCTOR MARC: No problem. It's why I went into medicine.

PATIENT: Hello, doctor. Three weeks ago I had a five-pound baby boy. I have a seven-pound bowling ball. Is that O.K.?
DOCTOR MARC: Huh? . . .

PATIENT: Can I go bowling?

DOCTOR MARC: What? Is this a word problem? How fast is the baby moving?

PATIENT: Bowling, I want to go bowling. My baby was five pounds and my ball is seven. Is it safe to bowl?

DOCTOR MARC: As long as you use the ball and not the baby.

PATIENT: I was just wondering, where do all the boogers go?

DOCTOR MARC: It's in the song: Where do all the boogers go, long time passing . . . Sing the song, you'll find out.

PATIENT: I'm about to have sex. What does syphilis look like on a penis?

DOCTOR MARC: Whoa! If you have to ask, just leave now. Just put on your clothes and walk out of the room.

PATIENT (from Zimbabwe): I have a yeast infection that's really bothering me.

DOCTOR MARC: How long has it been bothering you?

PATIENT: Since the War of Independence.

DOCTOR MARC: And since our War of Independence was over 200 years ago, I assume you are talking about the Zimbabwean War of Independence?

PATIENT: Yes.

DOCTOR MARC: I haven't been reading the papers lately. That would have been when?

PATIENT: Nineteen seventy-eight.

DOCTOR MARC: I see. Well, we all make sacrifices for our country.

While patients can make some foolish phone calls, physicians who are patients are often the most annoying. Karen just expects more from them. All first-time mothers are told to call the doctor when the contractions are five minutes apart. One soon-to-be Mom who was also a doctor called early in the evening:

PATIENT: My contractions are 20 minutes apart.
KAREN: Well, call back when they are five minutes apart.
Around midnight she woke us:
PATIENT: My contractions are only 15 minutes apart.
KAREN: As I said, call back when they are five minutes apart.
In the wee hours, the phone rang:
PATIENT: I think they are about 10 minutes apart now.
KAREN: Do you want to go to the hospital?
PATIENT: Should I?
KAREN: Usually we don't tell you to go in until the contractions are five minutes apart. That's what I've been saying.
PATIENT: OK. I'll wait.

At about 6:30 in the morning, Karen got a call from the hospital that this patient was in the hospital, was complete and ready to push. Karen scurried to the hospital in time for the delivery. Afterwards she asked the woman why she had gone to the hospital without calling. The woman replied, "I didn't want to bother you."

One Conclusion

So. That's what the life of an OB/GYN is all about. A laugh a minute. Well, maybe not completely. What you just read was the condensed, highlighted version. I took out some of the boring and routine of everyday practice. I had to, otherwise the mystique is ruined and I got no book. They do the same thing on TV. Like the show *E.R.*

My wife and I were watching one night and Karen piped in about her experience in the E.R. She said a typical night does not have quite the excitement or the activity of the hourlong drama that portrays it. Mostly, she said, it's people walking in and whining, "I've got a spider bite." Or, "I haven't pooped in five days." Or, her favorite:

PATIENT: I've got a stomach ache.
DOCTOR: Well, when did you last eat?
PATIENT: Here in the ER.
DOCTOR: And what did you have?
PATIENT: Cheese Doodles from the machine.
DOCTOR: I think I've solved your problem.

I couldn't watch *E.R.* after that. I kept thinking about the reality. The reality is not going to be an Emmy-winning episode, I can assure you. I'm not saying that all the exciting events on TV and in this book didn't happen, I just don't want it to be taken out of context.

I also don't want to give short shrift to the drama of the medical profession. This book has dealt with the lighter side of obstetrics and gynecology. We all know that this work can be excruciatingly serious. Karen's ability to joke about troubling things does not override the seriousness with which she takes her job and the feelings she develops for her patients. Her popularity as a physician stems in large part from the fact that she is truly caring. While she chose her specialty in part because it's mostly dealing with healthy people and the joyous occasion of having a baby, there are times when patients face tragic illness and death. These are harder situations to find humor in, but it does happen.

While a resident, Karen became very attached to one of her patients, a sweet woman in her 80s who had terminal ovarian cancer. Mrs. DiBiasio treated Karen like a granddaughter, even though she had trouble remembering her name. Karen was still going by her maiden name professionally, so she was called Dr. Regan, and Mrs. D. could only remember that it sounded like one of the presidents. She would call Karen "Doctor Roosevelt" or "Doctor Truman."

The two had developed such a bond during Mrs. D's final weeks that Karen wanted to make sure she was immediately notified when Mrs. D. died, no matter what time of day or night. It was unusual for us to get calls in the middle of the night when Karen was a resident, as being on call meant spending the full night in the hospital whether there were patients or not. So when the phone shrilled, I reached in the darkness to stop it from waking Karen at 2:30 in the morning.

It was the hospital calling.

A busy hospital operator's voice relayed the information. "Hospital calling for Dr. Regan to let her know that Mrs. DiBiasio died, could you hold on a second?"

Before I could absorb the information, I was on hold and the Muzak was in my ear. As I realized what was said and that I would have to relay this sad news to Karen, an upbeat, swinging Barry Manilow came on singing, "At the Copa/ Copacabaaana/ Music and passion were always in fashion . . . ." The operator was back. Unaware of my little musical interlude, she picked up in a somber voice right where she left off. "Sorry. Yes, Mrs. DiBiasio died about 10 minutes ago, and Dr. Regan, oops, hold on again . . . ." The music again, "Her name was Lola/She was a show girl . . . ."

I told Karen the news. She had realized immediately when the phone rang what it was. As much as she was prepared for it happening, Karen was still very sad. She went for a long walk. When she came back we talked for a bit. At some point I told her about the ridiculous musical interlude while I was being given the news. Karen laughed. At first she suggested that the hospital screen its Muzak, but on second thought she conjured up a whole service whereby upbeat tunes could be used by doctors when they have to transmit bad news to their patients. Something like "Itsy Bitsy Teeny Weeny Yellow Polka Dot Bikini" could get you bopping your head during the news of an abnormal Pap smear. It wasn't very high-minded humor, but it made me feel better to see Karen dealing with Mrs. D's death so well.

In the 12 years since Mrs. DiBiasio's death, I have met many OB/GYNs. I'm sure that most of them are wonderful doctors. I can't imagine any of them having more compassion for their patients than Karen does. Just as important, I know that none of them could have a better sense of humor about themselves or their work than my wife does about hers. She has a serious profession where life-determining issues are confronted daily. Might as well laugh your way through it. After all, eventually we all end up at the Copacabana.

Acknowledgments

I always thought that acknowledgments were like the author's chance to give an Academy Award acceptance speech and thank everyone they have ever known in thirty seconds. I would say that "I want to thank all the little people," but only the director of the Wizard of Oz could have said that without sounding trite. The following are all big people in the process of bringing this book to fruition. In no particular order of importance of their contribution, I must give my deepest thanks to:

All the doctors, midwives and nurses who contributed stories. I would thank you all by name, but I'm sure you'd rather I didn't. I also apologize for not corresponding with those who sent stories over the internet. An unfortunate computer crash eliminated all the e-mail addresses.

My agent, Caroline Carney, who was also an able and insightful editor.

My manager, (why I need an agent *and* a manager I don't know) Doreen Nakamura, who for some crazy reason still has big plans for me even though I don't pay her enough to cover our phone calls.

Jane O'Boyle for her consistent encouragement and help.

All who helped in the business or production aspects of putting the book together including: Anne Fahey, Mark Hoffman, Joyce Graham, Pamela Zoslov, Marissa Maslar, and Joe Gelles.

Everyone who read the book at varying stages and gave me suggestions even if the suggestion was to "Stop writing, now!"

Ron Lolich for hitting a grand slam with two outs in the ninth to beat the Red Sox 8-7 at an Indians game I was at back in the mid 70's. It has nothing to do with this book, but what a thrill it was for me, and I would never get a chance to thank him otherwise.

My mother and father who instilled in me the value such that if I wasn't going to be a doctor, at least I should marry one.

The star of the book, my dear wife Karen, who, I'm hoping, will one day give me permission to have this published.

About The Author

Marc Jaffe walks five miles to work each day, in the snow, just so he can write comedy. This is a little odd since he has an office in his home in Cleveland, but we all have our neuroses. Work of Marc's that you may have come across include: several Seinfeld episodes — most memorably the episode where Elaine accidentally exposes her nipple in a Christmas card; his nationally syndicated weekly humor column "The Quiz and Stuff"; his stand-up comedy performances on numerous TV shows and comedy club stages around the country; or by unwittingly hearing his voice on any of hundreds of radio and television commercials.

Marc is raising three daughters with only one wife to support him. When not reveling in the joys of family, Marc finds solace in the music of Thelonius Monk, yard work, and fervent worship of the Cleveland Indians.